THE MUSTARD SEED

The Story of St. Clare's Mercy Hospital

THE MUSTARD SEED

The Story of St. Clare's Mercy Hospital

Kathrine E. Bellamy, RSM

Flanker Press Ltd.
St. John's
2010

Library and Archives Canada Cataloguing in Publication

Bellamy, Kathrine E., 1923-2010
The mustard seed: the story of St. Clare's Mercy Hospital / Kathrine E. Bellamy.

Includes bibliographical references and index.
ISBN 978-1-897317-73-0

1. St. Clare's Mercy Hospital (St. John's, N.L.)--History. 2. Sisters of Mercy of Newfoundland--History. I. Title.

RA983.S362B44 2010   362.1109718'1   C2010-900579-1

PRINTED IN CANADA

Mixed Sources
Cert no. SW-COC-001271
© 1996 FSC
FSC

THE TEXT OF THIS BOOK IS PRINTED ON ANCIENT FOREST FRIENDLY PAPER, FSC CERTIFIED, THAT IS CHLORINE-FREE AND 100% POST CONSUMER WASTE.

FLANKER PRESS
P.O. BOX 2522, STATION C
ST. JOHN'S, NL A1C 6K1 CANADA
TOLL-FREE: 1-866-739-4420
WWW.FLANKERPRESS.COM

Cover Design: Adam Freake

14 13 12 11 10   2 3 4 5 6 7 8 9

Canada Council   Conseil des Arts
for the Arts   du Canada

We acknowledge the financial support of: the Government of Canada through the Book Publishing Industry Development Program (BPIDP); the Canada Council for the Arts which last year invested $20.1 million in writing and publishing throughout Canada; the Government of Newfoundland and Labrador, Department of Tourism, Culture and Recreation.

The Parable of the Mustard Seed

The kingdom of heaven is like a mustard seed that someone took and sowed in his field; it is the smallest of all seeds, but when it is grown it is the greatest of shrubs and becomes a tree, so that the birds of the air come and make nests in its branches.
—Matthew 13:31–32 (New Revised Standard Version)

Contents

PREFACE

The Story of St. Clare's Mercy Hospital

Let us haste to write down the stories and traditions of the people before they are forgotten.

—Henri-Raymond Casgrain,
Les Soirées Canadiennes (1861–1865)

When Bishop Michael Anthony Fleming decided to establish the Sisters of Mercy in Newfoundland, he had in mind not only the education of youth, but also the care of the sick. The story of the efforts of the sisters to fulfill this mandate of the bishop is the subject matter of this book.

The nest of buildings on LeMarchant Road and St. Clare Avenue in St. John's that make up St. Clare's Mercy Hospital is the most visible symbol of the contribution of the Sisters of Mercy to health care in Newfoundland. Since their arrival in Newfoundland on June 3, 1842, in addition to education, the Sisters of Mercy have embraced ministry to persons who are sick or in need as their special vocation.

Long before St. Clare's Mercy Hospital became a reality, the Sisters of Mercy went to the homes of the sick, caring for children suffering from a severe epidemic of measles in 1842, tending people suffering from typhus in St. John's Hospital in 1847, and caring for those suffering and dying at home in the cholera epidemics in 1854 and 1856. After school hours and on Sundays, the Sisters of Mercy regularly visited those afflicted by tuberculosis and other diseases at home, bringing both physical and spiritual comfort. The regular visitations to the General Hospital on Forest Road, to the Sanatorium, to the Hospital for

ix

Mental and Nervous Diseases, and to the Home for the Aged
and Infirm (known colloquially as the "Poor House") were all
part and parcel of the weekly routine of the Sisters of Mercy in
St. John's.

This was no less true for sisters stationed in the outports.
Visitation and relief of the sick and elderly were part and parcel
of the life of every sister. During the Spanish Influenza epidemic
on the West Coast, the Sisters of Mercy in St. George's and in
Curling were tireless in their efforts to relieve the suffering.
Although none of the sisters at that time had received specialized
medical training, they cared for the sick as best they could, wash-
ing the clothes and bedding of the sick, bringing soup and nour-
ishing food from the convent kitchens to hasten recovery, and
when death occurred—as happened all too frequently—offering
hope and consolation to the bereaved. All of this is fully docu-
mented in the Archives of the Sisters of Mercy of Newfoundland.
As well, contemporary newspapers carried accounts of the efforts
of the Sisters of Mercy to relieve the suffering of those afflicted by
the various epidemics that occurred from time to time in
Newfoundland.

Thus, it was inevitable, that when the opportunity came
for a more professional approach to caring for the sick, the
Sisters of Mercy eagerly embraced it. The opening of St.
Clare's Mercy Hospital on May 21, 1922, saw the fulfillment of
Bishop Fleming's dream and the beginning of the most visible
expression of the Mercy vocation to care for the sick.

There are few sources that record the early days of St.
Clare's Mercy Hospital. Other than newspaper accounts of
important events involving the hospital, most of the information
available is found in an unpublished manuscript written by Sr.
M. Fabian Hennebury entitled "St. Clare's Mercy Hospital,
1922–1982." The Archives of the Sisters of Mercy contain some
relevant material. Other sources, gathered from memories of the
sister-nurses who lived and worked at St. Clare's, are contained

in booklets printed to commemorate various anniversaries of the hospital, entitled *Historical Highlights.* Sr. M. Calasanctius Power wrote an historical account of the school of nursing in a privately printed document entitled, "The St. Clare's Mercy Hospital School of Nursing, 1939–1979."

However, after the establishment of the board of governors in 1956, a complete history of events at St. Clare's can be traced in the carefully kept minutes of the meetings of this board. In addition, the annual reports of St. Clare's Mercy Hospital record day-to-day events in the life of the hospital. Also, the late Sr. Catherine Kenny, former director of the school of nursing, made an invaluable contribution to St. Clare's by her careful preservation of pictures and artifacts relating to the hospital and the school of nursing. I have relied heavily on these sources in writing the story of St. Clare's.

Now that the work is finished, I look back with gratitude to the many people who provided advice and assistance as I went about my task. First of all, I thank the congregational archivist for the Sisters of Mercy of Newfoundland, Sr. Madonna Gatherall, RSM, for her uncomplaining and inexhaustible patience with my many requests; for the countless hours she spent looking up information, reading the manuscript, and making corrections; and for her invaluable suggestions. I offer my sincere gratitude to Mrs. Jackie Walsh, director of heritage and archives for the Congregation of the Sisters of Mercy. Jackie spared neither time nor trouble in checking and re-checking scraps of information, verifying the dates of important events in the life of the hospital, and providing many of the pictures used in the book. I am indebted to Sr. Marie Michael Power, former archivist for the Sisters of Mercy, for her meticulous documentation of available resources. I need to express gratitude to successive leadership teams of the Congregation of the Sisters of Mercy for their encouragement and for allowing me the time and space to pursue this kind of research. There are a number of other people who have assisted me in my search for information: Sr. M. Perpetua Kennedy, PBVM; Larry Dohey, Archives of the Archdiocese of St. John's; Sr. Paula Marlin, RSM, of the Sisters of Mercy in Baltimore, USA; Mrs. Bernadette Weinheber, RN, who provided stories from St. Clare's school of nursing; and Mrs. Harriet Doyle, RN, who provided valuable information on the school of nursing. I want to thank the members of my community at Our Lady of Mercy Convent for patiently accepting my irregular comings and goings as I hunted for information in many different places, and for tolerating my frequent lapses into silence as I struggled to make sense out of small, incomplete, and often contradictory scraps of information.

My hope and prayer is that all who read this book may share my admiration for and gratitude to those Sisters of Mercy who, working with dedicated professionals in the field of health care, brought the "mustard seed" that was planted in 1922 to full growth as one of the major health care institutions in Newfoundland and Labrador—St. Clare's Mercy Hospital.

Sr. M. Bernard Gladney,
RN, administrator

Sr. M. Gabriel Fleming

Sr. M. Catherine Greene

The first three Sisters of Mercy on the staff of St. Clare's Mercy Hospital, May 1922 to September 1922

EARLY DAYS

Great physicians and nurses, skilled and caring, intervened in my life and probably saved it.

—Senator John Kerry

The story of health care in Newfoundland dates back many years prior to the first Europeans setting foot on the island. We know that human beings lived here centuries before John Cabot set forth on his historic journey across the Atlantic. Although very little is known about the practices of the Aboriginal peoples of Newfoundland, there is no doubt that they had their own methods for dealing with illnesses and injuries.

They understood which plants were edible and which were poisonous. Medical procedures revolved around the use of local herbs in teas, poultices, and other preparations. Sweating and fasting were also believed to alleviate certain illnesses, although documentation of the specific cures and their origins is scarce.[1]

Probably the first medical person to set foot on the island of Newfoundland was a Genoese barber-surgeon whom John Cabot took along with him on his voyage of discovery.[2] Even after permanent settlement took place on the

1. Jenny Higgins, "19th-Century Health Care," Newfoundland and Labrador Heritage, http://www.heritage.nf.ca/society/19c_health.html.

2. Stephen Nolan, *A History of Health Care in Newfoundland and Labrador* (St. John's: Newfoundland and Labrador Health and Community Services Archive and Museum, 2004), 1.

island, there were no resident doctors. Many settlers never saw a medical practitioner and those who were lucky enough to do so had access to medical services only between spring and fall when fishing fleets from the West Country of England or naval patrols were in port. For the rest of the year, and that meant during the harshest months of winter and early spring, people were on their own.[3]

However, these early Newfoundlanders were not without their own brand of resourcefulness and ingenuity, coupled with folk remedies inherited from English and Irish ancestors, and mixed in with a certain amount of superstition. A number of home cures were used to help the sick and injured. In addition, people began to understand and appreciate "the medicinal purposes of the natural resources around them and to create solutions for many of the medical problems that plagued them."[4]

Right from the beginning, settlers were accompanied or followed by missionaries of different faiths, eager to bring the message of the Gospel to this lonely little island. But before they could do this, they had to take into account the physical needs of the people to whom they hoped to minister. Stephen Nolan, in his book *A History of Health Care in Newfoundland and Labrador*, wrote:

Early missionaries soon discovered that before they could begin the delicate process of saving people's immortal souls, they would have to save their prospective converts' ailing bodies. There was little point in converting a flock whose members died, so the missionaries had to become adept at the art of healing to ensure success for their missions.[5]

3. John F. O'Mara, "I Swear by Apollo: Irish Physicians and Surgeons in Newfoundland and Labrador before 1900" (lecture, Irish Newfoundland Association, St. John's, November 17, 2002), 19.
4. Nolan, *A History of Health Care*, 28.
5. Ibid., 35.

This conviction was shared by missionaries of all denominations. Priests and clergy of all faiths were assiduous in their care for the sick, first and foremost because they were moved to compassion at the sight of suffering and pain.[6] While they did their best to address each and every situation of physical injury or illness, at the same time they brought spiritual comfort and consolation by proclaiming the message of Christ's saving love. Thus, in the early days, for the most part, physical healing and religious teaching went hand in hand, something that was clearly embraced by the head of the Roman Catholic Church in Newfoundland, Bishop Michael Anthony Fleming.

One example of Bishop Fleming's concern for the health and well-being of his flock occurred in the summer and fall of 1835 when an epidemic of smallpox swept through St. John's. That year over six thousand cases were officially reported in the town.[7] Bishop Fleming was furious over the failure of the government to act to alleviate the sufferings of the people, especially of the poor, but in spite of his anxiety to help his people, he was handicapped in his efforts because of his own ill health at the time. Nevertheless, he did what he could, principally by publicly complaining of the failure of the government to check the disease. By November, the epidemic had just about run its course in St. John's, but it broke out in the nearby fishing village of Petty Harbour. Bishop Fleming, realizing how impossible it was for the residents of the village to receive any medical aid, bought a cow, packed up his bags and set out for Petty Harbour with the cow trotting along behind him. In his book, *Fire Upon the Earth*, Brother J. B. Darcy recorded what happened:

---

6. This statement is confirmed by the number of medical textbooks from the libraries of early Roman Catholic priests. These books are preserved in the Archives of the Archdiocese of St. John's.

7. Brother J. B. Darcy, *Fire Upon the Earth: The Life and Times of Bishop Michael Fleming, O.S.F.* (St. John's: Creative Book Publishing, 2003), 92.

He [Bishop Fleming] had by now acquired a basic understanding of the disease through the instruction of the doctors and through his care for the sick in St. John's, so he immediately set out for Petty Harbour taking with him his medical chest and a cow to provide the sufferers with fresh milk. He . . . set up residence and a dispensary in an empty hut near the church . . . Here he remained for the winter, caring for the sick and making no distinction between Catholic and Protestant. As a result of his ministrations, when the disease had abated in February, only two deaths had occurred out of 400 severe cases.[8]

As he worked and struggled to alleviate the sufferings of the sick poor, Fleming realized that education was the answer to many of the problems that plagued his flock. He saw that one of the best ways to ensure the health and well-being of the Catholic population was to provide schooling for young girls, for if the mothers of future generations were well-educated themselves, Fleming reasoned, they would appreciate the benefits derived from education and ensure that their children received similar advantages. To that end, Bishop Fleming established the Congregation of the Presentation Sisters in St. John's in 1833. The mandate of the sisters was to provide a basic education for poor girls so that they would learn how to care for their families and become self-sufficient, contributing members of society.

His plan to introduce the Presentation Sisters succeeded beyond his most optimistic expectations. Within a very short time, their schools were crowded. Well pleased with this success, Bishop Fleming turned his attention to another problem that had exercised his patience and troubled his conscience for many years. In a letter to Archbishop O'Connell of Dublin, the bishop wrote:

---

8. Ibid., 93–94.

I saw that so far I had only provided for the religious instruction of a portion of my people, and I sighed over the wants of the more respectable, the more wealthy, and comfortable classes because the want of good female schools even for these was deplorable . . . and therefore I determined, as the means best calculated to accomplish this end, to introduce a community of nuns of the Order of Mercy whose rule would permit them to keep a pension school.[9]

Lack of educational opportunities for the more affluent members of his flock was not the only motive that inspired Bishop Fleming to turn to Catherine McAuley, foundress of the Sisters of Mercy, for an answer to his problem. The compassionate bishop felt keenly the sufferings of the sick poor among his flock who were vulnerable to the various epidemics of typhus and other contagious diseases that frequently afflicted the citizens of St. John's. Thus, the advantage of introducing into his diocese a community of women religious who were not bound by enclosure and whose rule identified the visitation and care of the sick as one of their main duties was not lost on Bishop Fleming.[10]

Having resolved to establish a convent of the Sisters of Mercy in St. John's, the bishop went to Dublin in 1838, visited Catherine McAuley at the convent on Baggot Street and secured her commitment to a foundation in his diocese. At the same time, the foundress agreed to accept into the novitiate a young Irish lady who had lived in St. John's for several years. This young lady, Marianne Creedon, was familiar with conditions in St. John's and was anxious to dedicate her life in service to the poor,

---

9. Bishop Michael Anthony Fleming to Archbishop O'Connell, February 19, 1844, Letters on the State of Religion in Newfoundland, 103/2/27, Archives of the Archdiocese of St. John's (hereafter cited as Letters, AASJ).

10. Bishop Fleming to Monsignor De Luca, April 2, 1842, Letters, 103/3/28, AASJ.

the sick, and the uneducated as a Sister of Mercy. Sponsored by Bishop Fleming, Marianne Creedon was received into the Convent of the Sisters of Mercy at Baggot Street, Dublin, on July 4, 1839. The plan was that when her novitiate training had been completed, Marianne Creedon would return to St. John's and establish a Convent of Mercy there.[11]

Bishop Fleming was in Ireland from December 1841 until April 1842.[12] While he was there, plans for the Newfoundland mission were finalized and arrangements made for the sisters to travel to St. John's. In a letter to Monsignor De Luca in Rome, the bishop wrote, "I have booked passage on a vessel to bring to Newfoundland a community of Nuns of the Order of Mercy . . . for the education of the rich and for the assistance of the sick and the indigent."[13] On May 2, 1842, Marianne Creedon (now Sr. Mary Francis), Sr. M. Rose Lynch, and Sr. M. Ursula Frayne left Ireland. They arrived in St. John's the following month, on Friday, June 3, 1842.

---

11. Bishop Fleming to Archbishop O'Connell, February 19, 1844, Letters, 103/2/27, AASJ.

12. The author is indebted to Brother J. B. Darcy, CFC, for Bishop Fleming's chronology.

13. Bishop Fleming to Monsignor De Luca, April 2, 1842, Letters, 103/3/38, AASJ.

THE SISTERS OF MERCY AND CARE OF THE SICK

Real compassion comes from seeing the suffering of others. You feel a sense of responsibility, and you want to do something for them.

—The Dalai Lama

After their arrival, the sisters took two days to settle into their new home, but, with the impatience of youth, they were anxious to begin their work without any delay. A few weeks later Bishop Fleming wrote, "They [the Sisters of Mercy] are now actively engaged in their sacred employ, daily visiting the sick. Indeed so pressing were they to be permitted to enter upon their labours immediately on their arrival, I was obliged to consent to it on the subsequent Monday."[1]

The sisters did not have to wait long for a serious challenge to their skill in nursing the sick. The weather in the month of July 1842 turned hot and humid, creating the ideal conditions for an outbreak of one of the epidemics that swept through St. John's at regular intervals. The *Patriot* reported:

The Measles still prevails among us and though not so generally as it did some weeks past, as yet retains its force with a tenacity for which this disease is so characteristic. The

1. Bishop Fleming to Rev. and Dear Sir, Feast of St. John [June 24], 1842, Letters, 103/1/8, AASJ. The address "Rev. and Dear Sir" was the customary manner of addressing a clergyman in Ireland. The recipient in this case is unknown but was most likely Archbishop Daniel Murray of Dublin.

intense heat of the weather, though it has been oppressive to the hale and hearty, has favoured the patient labouring under this disorder . . . The *Sisters of Mercy*—introduced here by that noble Philanthropist, the Right Rev. Dr. Fleming, have ministered with untiring zeal among the poor afflicted, from the very moment of their arrival, and never, we believe, was there a greater need for their hallowed services than at this period. But it is when sickness is prevalent—when disease is raging—when death hovers round—that those Sisters—like "Angels of Mercy"—flit from one scene of misery to another, administering to the wants of those who otherwise might suffer without assistance and die for want of it.[2]

Although one of Bishop Fleming's main reasons for bringing the Sisters of Mercy to St. John's was to educate the daughters of the more affluent Catholics, Our Lady of Mercy School was not ready to receive students until May 1, 1843. Thus, during the first eleven months after their arrival in St. John's, the Sisters of Mercy spent their time visiting the sick poor in their homes. Even after the school opened, the sisters did not consider themselves dispensed from their duty of caring for the sick. Every day after school and on weekends, they carried out their ministry of visitation to those who were so much in need of their care. In the meantime, the sisters were joined by another young woman, Maria Nugent, who was professed as a Sister of Mercy on March 25, 1843, and given the name Sr. Mary Joseph. With this encouragement, Bishop Fleming, who was never shy of dreaming impossible dreams, decided that he would expand their ministry to the sick:

Until the pious Sisterhood of Mercy, judiciously and usefully augmented, shall become capable of attending, not only to . . . the duty of continuing to soothe the pallet of

---

2. *Patriot and Terra Nova Herald*, August 3, 1842, 3.

the wretched and diseased in the abodes of the poor, as well as in the hospital, which it will be my care to add to that happy institution, I shall not consider my mission accomplished.[3]

However, this was one plan that Bishop Fleming had to abandon. The undertaking that had begun with such promise on June 3, 1842, faltered and would have collapsed except for the courage and determination of one of the three pioneer Sisters of Mercy, Sr. M. Francis Creedon. In November 1843, after only seventeen months in Newfoundland, two of the original three missionaries, Sr. M. Ursula Frayne and Sr. M. Rose Lynch, returned to Ireland. The two remaining sisters, Sr. M. Francis Creedon and Sr. M. Joseph Nugent, continued the ceaseless demands of teaching in the school and caring for the sick poor in their homes and at St. John's Hospital, which was about an hour's walk from Mercy Convent.

In late May 1847, as a consequence of an epidemic of typhus that broke out in St. John's, the two Sisters of Mercy were forced to close the school so that they might devote all their time to caring for the sick. By June 3, thirty-six patients were crowded into the small ward at St. John's Hospital, each one requiring all the attention and skill the sisters could bring. It was almost inevitable that the frail Sr. M. Joseph Nugent would fall victim to the contagion. No amount of medical skill or loving care was effective in halting the progress of the infection. Sr. M. Joseph died on June 17, 1847, leaving Sr. M. Francis Creedon to carry on the mission alone. For ten long months, she struggled to fulfill her ministry, reopening Our Lady of Mercy School and visiting the sick and dying until, in April 1848, she accepted her first postulant, Agnes Nugent. A short time later, two other young women were accepted and professed as Sisters of Mercy in St. John's. The tide had

3. Bishop Fleming to Dr. O'Connell, fifth letter, February 19, 1844, Letters, 103/2/27, AASJ.

turned! From that point on, the Mercy congregation grew and expanded over the years, spreading throughout Newfoundland and Labrador, and even as far as Peru.

Meanwhile, Bishop Fleming himself was suffering from the illness that would claim his life a few years later. He died on July 12, 1850, and his dream of building a Catholic hospital under the direction of the Sisters of Mercy seems to have been forgotten by his immediate successors. It would be more than seventy years before Bishop Fleming's vision of a Mercy hospital in St. John's would be realized.

The years passed, but there was no further mention of establishing a Catholic hospital in St. John's. Nevertheless, the Sisters of Mercy were always present whenever misfortune, sickness, or death visited the people to whom they had dedicated their lives in service.

An outbreak of cholera in North America and the West Indies during the spring of 1854 caused the Newfoundland government to impose quarantine on all ships arriving from these countries. But in spite of this precaution, several deaths from the infection were reported during August of that year and by October the full fury of the epidemic broke. Fortunately, the contagion did not spread to areas outside St. John's, but during the last three months of 1854, a total of more than five hundred deaths were reported in St. John's. Aware of how many were dying in the hospital, people who became ill insisted on remaining at home, thus unwittingly contributing to the spread of the disease.[4]

In light of the seriousness of the epidemic, the sisters closed Our Lady of Mercy School from the end of July 1854 until January 1855.[5] As the disease spread through the centre

---

4. *Encyclopedia of Newfoundland and Labrador*, s.v. "Health."

5. There are no entries in the accounts book of the Convent of Our Lady of Mercy recording the paying of school fees from July 30 to December 10, 1854, when an entry, "due February 23, 1855" was recorded. School fees were received again in January 1855.

of the town, the four Sisters of Mercy[6] found themselves in constant attendance on the sick and the dying. They provided food, medicine, and comfort. Their presence was a sign of hope when even close relatives and friends, for fear of contagion, left the stricken family members to cope as best they could.[7] A local historian, Paul O'Neill, wrote of the efforts of the Sisters of Mercy during this epidemic as follows:

> It was during this terrible epidemic that the few Mercy nuns then in St. John's distinguished themselves by going into cholera-ridden homes to tend the helplessly sick and haul out corpses that nobody else would touch so that they could be placed in coffins that were dumped on the streets.[8]

In response to the number of orphans left by this and similar epidemics, the Sisters of Mercy opened the first orphanage for girls in Newfoundland on December 8, 1854. The orphanage, adjoining Mercy Convent, was paid for from funds left to the Sisters of Mercy by Bishop Fleming for this purpose. Five years later, the orphans and the sisters who cared for them moved to St. Michael's Orphanage, Belvedere.

After a brief period of relative freedom from serious epidemics, in 1856, St. John's was hit again by another outbreak of cholera. Once more, the sisters at Mercy Convent hastened to the aid of families stricken by disease and death. Their experience in the 1854 epidemic had prepared them for this emergency. In his book, *The Ecclesiastical History of*

---

6. Sr. M. Francis Creedon, Sr. M. Vincent (Agnes) Nugent, Sr. M. Xavier Bernard, and Sr. M. Elizabeth Regan were the only four Sisters of Mercy in Newfoundland at the time.

7. Mary Austin Carroll, *Leaves from the Annals of the Sisters of Mercy*, vol. 3, *Newfoundland and the United States* (New York: Catholic Publication Society, 1883), 27.

8. Paul O'Neill, *The Oldest City: The Story of St. John's, Newfoundland* (Portugal Cove-St. Philip's, NL: Boulder Publications, 2003), 233.

Kathrine E. Bellamy, RSM

Newfoundland, Archbishop Michael F. Howley paid tribute to the work of the Sisters of Mercy during this time of crisis:

> In the year 1856 the cholera broke out in St. John's and raged with great violence. Then were seen the Sisters of Mercy in their element. From daylight to dark, and often through the night, they worked indefatigably. No part of the city slums was too dark or too filthy for them. They entered the houses of the plague-stricken when all others had abandoned them, lighting the fires and preparing some humble food; scrubbing and cleaning up the little tenements dressing and washing the sick; and finally, carrying the dead bodies to the coffins, which were placed at the doors on the streets by fearful officials.[9]

There were only five Sisters of Mercy at Mercy Convent at the time, the intrepid Sr. M. Francis Creedon having died the year before (1855) at the age of forty-three years. Two of the five were native-born Newfoundlanders: Sr. M. Baptist Tarahan and Sr. M. Clare Tarahan, daughters of Thomas and Mary Tarahan of St. Johns. Later, Sr. M. Clare Tarahan was to give her life while nursing sick children at St. Michael's Orphanage, Belvedere, during the cholera outbreak of 1872.

It appears that, through the years, the Sisters of Mercy carried on regular visitation and care of the sick at St. John's Hospital. In a submission to the Government of Newfoundland, Bishop Mullock complained about conditions at the hospital and referred to the ministry of the Sisters of Mercy. The *Journal of the House of Assembly* has the following entry:

> Mr. Talbot presented a petition from the Right Reverend Dr. Mullock, Roman Catholic Bishop of St. John's, which was received setting forth:—

9. Very Reverend M. F. Howley, *Ecclesiastical History of Newfoundland* (Boston: Doyle and Whittle, 1888), 376.

12

That the horrible state of St. John's Hospital is a disgrace to the community and a source of pestilence to the entire people. That typhus fever is so fixed in it that no one can approach it without danger of death. That most of those whom accidents or other diseases oblige to have recourse to the Hospital get typhus fever while there; and the quarantine now enforced against all vessels from St. John's to Spain is caused by this fact, and it is probable that it will be put in force by other nations also, as St. John's is acquiring the character of a permanently infected port. That already three Catholic Clergymen have got typhus by attending the patients in said Hospital, two of whom died; several Sisters of Mercy and two Protestant Clergymen also got the same sickness while on duty.[10]

Long before the Roman Catholic ecclesiastical authorities were in a position to address the establishment of a Catholic hospital on the island, the Sisters of Mercy cared for the sick in different places throughout Newfoundland. As a matter of fact, wherever the sisters established a convent in Newfoundland, the records show that they considered the visitation and care of the sick to be one of their principal duties. For example, toward the end of the First World War, Spanish Influenza broke out in Asia and Europe and was subsequently brought to Newfoundland by soldiers returning from the war. When the people of St. George's fell ill, the sisters of St. Michael's Convent were quick to respond. Many years later, Sr. M. Xavier Wadden, a member of the community at the time, wrote an account of the tense days of the Spanish Influenza when so many people, especially the poor, were suffering and dying:

The Sisters in St. George's and Curling cared for the sick poor

---

10. *Journal of the House of Assembly*, Third Session of the Ninth General Assembly of Newfoundland, February 10, 1868, 18.

in their homes. All denominations were cared for during this epidemic that the people called, "The Bad 'Flu." It was in St. George's during the time (1918–1919) and the Sisters took turns visiting the sick. Bishop Power got the Court House fitted up as a temporary hospital. Long carts, covered by blankets, were fitted up to bring the sick to the "hospital." Father [Michael] O'Reilly (later Bishop) used to go the "hospital" in the early morning, long before Mass, to bring Holy Viaticum to the dying in the Court House Hospital. The Sisters took turns in the hospital during the day and in the early morning. We also visited the sick in their homes, bringing hot soup, clothing, etc. Every day we washed and dressed the children— these families were very poor. We visited one family, I remember, where the seven children were all stricken with the 'Flu. They were just lying around—the mother had died. While we were there the father [entered], coming from the woods where he was looking for rabbits to make soup for the children. No central heating in those days! [11]

When the epidemic spread to the Bay of Islands, the Sisters of Mercy at the Convent of St. Mary's on the Humber in Curling immediately volunteered their services. They visited and nursed the sick, irrespective of religious affiliation, brought food and clothing where necessary and prepared the dead for burial. When they were unable to care for the sick in their own homes, the sisters converted one of the classrooms in the school into a makeshift hospital. Day and night, assisted by other parishioners, they ministered to the needs of the sufferers.[12]

The importance of the ministry of the Sisters of Mercy to

---

11. Sr. M. Xavier Wadden, unpublished manuscript, MG 2/1/354, Archives of the Sisters of Mercy, St. John's (hereafter cited as ASMSJ).

12. Sr. M. Williamina Hogan, RSM, *Pathways of Mercy: History of the Foundation of the Sisters of Mercy in Newfoundland, 1842–1984* (St. John's: Harry Cuff Publications, 1986), 271.

the sick was not lost on the archbishop of St. John's, Michael F. Howley. Furthermore, the archbishop was aware that the establishment of a Catholic hospital in St John's was part of Bishop Fleming's plan for the Sisters of Mercy in Newfoundland. Archbishop Howley began to consider the possibility of establishing such a hospital in St. John's under the direction of the Sisters of Mercy. However, just as he was debating the merits of having a Catholic hospital in St. John's, the archbishop was presented with another pressing need—one that had far-reaching implications for the Sisters of Mercy.

A Home Away From Home

*The empowerment of women throughout the world cannot fail
to result in a more caring, tolerant, just and peaceful life for all.*
                                                    · —Aung San Suu Kyi

During the period immediately preceding the First World
War, a series of events occurred that caused Archbishop
Howley to consider the plight of young girls who came from
the outports to St. John's to find work. Strangely enough, the
Mercy Sisters themselves played no part in the transactions that
followed and that led eventually to the establishment of one of
their principal ministries in Newfoundland.

In the early years of the twentieth century, a large piece of
property on LeMarchant Road in St. John's came into the pos-
session of the Presentation Sisters of St. John's through Sr. M.
Clare Waldron, who had inherited the land on the death of her
brother, Father Thomas Waldron. In the early years, the
Presentation Sisters used the property called "Waldron's
Farm" as a grazing ground for cattle.[1] At a later date, the sisters
leased part of the Waldron property to the Honourable
Edward Michael Jackman, minister of finance for the
Newfoundland government, better known as "Jackman the
Tailor."[2] Jackman built a large, private home on his piece of
land, and called it, the "White House."

Some years later, another Presentation Sister by the name
of Sr. M. Clare English entered the picture. Sr. M. Clare was

1. O'Neill, *The Oldest City*, 247.
2. Ibid.

interested in providing a hostel for young girls who came from the outports to work in the city of St. John's.[3] To this end she had raised funds from the sale of knitted goods, the sale of cancelled stamps, school concerts, and donations from friends. It was a slow, tedious process, but Sr. M. Clare persevered. And then there occurred an event that must have seemed to her like a miracle. She received a visit from a man by the name of John Funchion who had been, at one time, a boarder in her mother's house on Water Street in St. John's. Funchion went to work in the Yukon during the time of the gold rush and, as a result, had become very wealthy. His purpose in returning to St. John's was to marry a lady who had been a childhood friend of Sr. M. Clare English. Shortly after the wedding, the bride and groom visited Sr. M. Clare at the Presentation Convent. During the visit, Funchion presented her with the gift of a rosary made of forty gold nuggets.[4]

At this point, the Knights of Columbus enter the story. In 1911, the supreme master of the fourth degree Knights of Columbus, John H. Reddin, came to St. John's and was introduced to Sr. M. Clare English. During their conversation, Sr. M. Clare asked Mr. Reddin to find a buyer who would be willing to pay one hundred dollars for the "Golden Rosary." The following year, the supreme knight, James A. Flaherty, visited St. John's and informed her that the Knights of Columbus wished to purchase the "Golden Rosary" as a gift to James Cardinal Gibbons of Baltimore on the occasion of his golden jubilee.[5] Sr. M. Clare accepted his proposal and to her astonishment and delight, he presented her with a cheque for one thousand dollars, a considerable sum of money in those days. This large sum of money, together with the funds she had collected through her small fundraising efforts, was enough to

---

3. It will be remembered that the same motive inspired Catherine McAuley to build the House of Mercy on Baggot Street in Dublin.

4. O'Neill, *The Oldest City*, 247.

5. Ibid.

permit Sr. M. Clare English to act on her dream of establishing a hostel for working girls. Before she could go any further, Archbishop Howley intervened.

There are two versions of what happened next. One account is found in Paul O'Neill's book, *The Oldest City*:

> She [Sr. M. Clare English] was called to a lengthy private meeting in the convent parlour with Archbishop Howley. When she returned to her room it was obvious from the crest-fallen look on her face that something unpleasant had transpired. She turned to her secretary and said, "Send it all to the Mercy Order." When the secretary protested . . . she was told it was the Archbishop's wish and she must obey. Despite the fact that Sister Clare had drawn from the prelate the promise that her original purpose would not be forgotten, the order seems to have come as a severe shock to her. Already in poor health, she began to fail and died shortly afterwards.[6]

On the other hand, at the opening of the hostel in September 1913, Archbishop Howley addressed the assembled guests as follows:

> For the past few years the matter of opening the "Home" . . . had been frequently mooted among the Sisters. The late Sister M. Clare English of the Presentation Order was particularly active about it. I gave her leave to receive for the purpose any

---

6. Ibid., 305. There are several puzzling statements in this account. 1) Sr. M. Clare was not the superior or in an administrative position, so it is very unlikely she would have had a secretary. 2) Because of her vow of poverty, any money that Sr. M. Clare had collected, even with the permission of the bishop, would not have been in her own possession but would have been under the care of the superior of the convent. 3) Again, because of her vow of poverty, Sr. M. Clare would not have been able to dispose of this money without the explicit permission of the superior. Therefore, the statement, "send it all to the Mercy Order," is inexplicable in the context of the time.

donation which might be offered to her . . . She had collected some three thousand dollars when she was called away to her reward without seeing the accomplishment of her most ardent desires. Though the amount collected was but mere trifle yet I determined, trusting in God's unbounded goodness, to commence the work. I had promised Sister M. Clare on her deathbed that the work on which she had set her heart should not be neglected.[7]

Early records of St. Clare's Mercy Hospital noted that Sr. M. Clare English requested "that the Home purchased by the Archbishop be placed under the direction of the Sisters of Mercy since, at that time, the Presentation Sisters were not involved in Social Work of this type."[8] In announcing that the new "Home" was to be under the direction of the Sisters of Mercy, Archbishop Howley alluded to the fact that in the rule of the Sisters of Mercy, the operation of such an institution was one of the ministries for which they had been founded.

Whatever the real facts of the matter, the archbishop acted on Sr. M. Clare's desire to establish a home for working girls. By adding to the amount Sr. M. Clare had received from the sale of the "Golden Rosary," Archbishop Howley bought the "White House" from E. M. Jackman for five thousand dollars with the objective of turning it into a hostel for young women who came to St. John's looking for work.

During the Christmas holidays, 1912, the archbishop visited the Sisters of Mercy at St. Bride's College, Littledale, where his friend Sr. M. Joseph Kelly was superior. But this was no ordinary visit. The archbishop was looking for volunteers to staff his new project, the Home for Working Girls.

---

7. Archbishop M. F. Howley, "St. Claire's [sic] Home for Girls," *Evening Telegram*, September 29, 1913, 5.

8. Sr. M. Fabian Hennebury, "St. Clare's Mercy Hospital, 1922–1982," unpublished manuscript, ASMSJ, 3–4.

Two sisters responded immediately: Sr. M. Rose Power and Sr. M. Bernard Gladney. Archbishop Howley chose Sr. M. Bernard Gladney from the Littledale staff, then he went to Mercy Convent, where he selected Sr. M. Berchmans Quinn as the person most suited for service in the proposed Home for Working Girls. Finally, he appointed Sr. M. Pius Mulcahy of St. Anne's Convent, Burin, to be the first superior of the hostel.

With the staff of the hostel in place, the archbishop turned his attention to making extensive renovations to the "White House" to convert it into a suitable residence for young women. He then appointed Sr. M. Pius Mulcahy and Sr. M. Bernard Gladney to supervise the renovations. Accordingly, the two sisters took up residence in St. Michael's Convent, Belvedere, so that they could be within walking distance of the new hostel. Every morning for six weeks, the two sisters walked across LeMarchant Road to the hostel, where they remained all day, returning to Belvedere in the evening. After alterations to the physical layout of the "White House" had been completed, the next task was to purchase the necessary materials—furniture, bedding, kitchen appliances, et cetera—to ensure the comfort and convenience of the residents. Finally, by the middle of September, everything was ready.

On the day the hostel was opened, the archbishop announced, "We give it the name of 'St. Clare's Home' as a reminder and an expression of gratitude to Sister M. Clare, who may be considered as its founder." [9] The Mercy Convent Annals pick up the story:

Saint Clare's Home in the city of St. John's was opened by His Grace, Archbishop Howley on the Feast of Saint Michael, the 29th of September in the year of our Lord, one thousand nine

---

9. Howley, "St. Claire's [sic] Home for Girls."

hundred and thirteen under the patronage of Our Blessed Lady of Mercy and the great Saint Clare, as a "Home for Working Girls."

The first Mass was celebrated in the little chapel of the Convent by His Grace, Archbishop Howley on that day.

The Sisters who went to establish this Convent were, Mother M. Pius Mulcahy, Mother Superior, Sister M. Berchmans Quinn, and Sister M. Bernard Gladney.[10]

Applications came in immediately. The first three residents were three young qualified stenographers, former residents of St. Michael's Orphanage, Belvedere. Other young women followed until the home was filled to capacity. A few older ladies applied, but only three could be accommodated. "Within the ten years that the 'Home' was in operation, ten religious vocations were developed. Four of these entered our own Mercy Congregation . . . six entered in communities in the U.S.A." [11]

Meanwhile, Archbishop Howley was being haunted by Bishop Fleming's vision of establishing a Catholic hospital in St. John's. But it seems that the archbishop needed something more than the dream of a long-dead predecessor before he would even consider establishing such an institution. The necessary incentive came through the action of a young doctor in St. John's.

In 1913 or 1914, just prior to the outbreak of the First World War, Dr. William Roberts, a native of St. John's,

10. Annals, Convent of Our Lady of Mercy, St. John's, ASMSJ.

11. *Mercy Communico*, St. Clare's Mercy Convent—St. Clare's Home for Working Girls—St. Clare's Mercy Hospital, RG 10/9/30, ASMSJ, 1. Creusa Giovannini was one of the young ladies who entered the Mercy congregation in Newfoundland. Throughout her religious life, she was known by her religious name, Sr. Mary Julien. The identity of the other three young ladies who entered the Sisters of Mercy in Newfoundland is unknown.

returned from Scotland to set up medical practice in his home-town. Dr. Roberts had specialized in the treatment of medical problems experienced by women, and in order to practise his specialty, he had adapted the top floor of his residence as a small hospital for women.[12]

Dr. Roberts's initiative prompted Archbishop Howley to act on Bishop Fleming's hope of establishing a hospital in St. John's to be administered by the Sisters of Mercy. But before he could do this, he needed nurses. In July 1914, on his way home from a visit to Rome, Howley visited the Mercy Hospital in Cork, Ireland, where he arranged for a Sister of Mercy from St. John's to begin nursing studies at that institution.[13] When he returned to St. John's, the archbishop visited Sr. M. Pius Mulcahy at St. Clare's Home and presented his idea to her. As soon as the archbishop had left, M. Pius hurried off to tell the news to her associates, Sr. M. Berchmans Quinn and Sr. M. Bernard Gladney. Sr. M. Berchmans, who was happy with her lot as a teacher, said nothing, but Sr. M. Bernard was overjoyed and offered herself immediately as a candidate for nurse's training. As it happened, it was just as well she had, for the archbishop had selected her already as the one to blaze this new trail in health care.[14] The archbishop also realized that he would have to begin the construction of a new building or find an existing structure that could be adapted for use as a hospi-tal. He decided that it was not possible to finance the construc-tion of a new facility, and so, after reviewing the buildings avail-able to him, he decided that St. Clare's Home for Working Girls could be adapted for use as a small Catholic hospital.

---

12. Joyce Nevitt, *White Caps and Black Bands: Nursing in Newfoundland to 1934.* (St. John's: Jesperson Press, 1978), 146.

13. Apparently, this was before the archbishop had discussed this plan with the Sisters of Mercy in St. John's. He seems to have taken for grant-ed their consent to administer and serve in his proposed hospital!

14. Sr. M. Francis Hickey, *Mercy Communico* (January 1969), RG 37/2/26, ASMSJ, 2.

Without further delay, he informed the sisters and the residents at St. Clare's of his plan. Sr. M. Bernard Gladney was told to pack her bags and prepare to leave for Ireland. Unfortunately for the archbishop's plans, the First World War broke out and it was considered unsafe for Sr. M. Bernard to travel across the Atlantic Ocean to begin her training as a nurse. And then, before any further steps could be taken, Archbishop Howley died on October 15, 1914. St. Clare's Home for Working Girls was safe for the time being.

FROM HOME TO HOSPITAL

There is nothing more difficult to take in hand, more perilous to conduct, or more uncertain in its success than to take the lead in the introduction of a new order to things.
— Niccolò Machiavelli, *The Prince*

Shortly after Archbishop Howley's death in October 1914, Sr. M. Pius Mulcahy, the superior of St. Clare's Home was appointed novice mistress at Littledale, and Sr. M. Bernard Gladney, who had by this time given up hope of becoming a nurse, was appointed superior of the home. The ministry to working women was continued but operated at a loss. Although it was meant to be self-supporting, the salaries of the young women who became residents were so small that a nominal amount of fifty cents a week was charged for room and board. It was clear that other programs would have to be introduced to provide enough income to keep the home in operation. A morning kindergarten class was opened for children in the area, and classes in business education—typing, shorthand, and accounting—were offered in the evening by Sr. M. Catherine Greene, who was assigned to St. Clare's to teach these courses. In addition, a music teacher, Sr. M. Gerard O'Reilly, was transferred from Mercy Convent to conduct lessons in music. Within a few weeks, forty-three pupils were receiving piano lessons. All this helped relieve the financial stress of managing the home. The sisters were able to continue to provide affordable housing to the grossly underpaid young ladies who were working in the various business establishments of St. John's. In fact, following these initiatives, the home was so successful that soon it was too small and many applicants had to be refused admission. The problem was presented to the new archbishop, Edward Patrick Roche, who immediately approved an addition to the building that provided, among other things, a new twelve-bed dormitory and a large dining room.[1]

Meanwhile, Archbishop Roche, who had been vicar general of the Archdiocese of St. John's during the final years of Howley's episcopate, had not forgotten his predecessor's plans to turn St. Clare's Home for Working Girls into a Catholic hospital. The First World War, which had prevented Sr. M. Bernard Gladney from going to Cork to train as a nurse, was coming to an end, and so Archbishop Roche decided that the time had come to act. In 1918, in consultation with Sr. M. Bridget O'Connor, mother general of the Sisters of Mercy, and much to Sr. M. Bernard's delight, he arranged for her to begin her nursing studies at Mercy Hospital in Pittsburgh, USA. In a letter to the superior of Mercy Hospital, the archbishop wrote:

Dear Sister Superior

The Mother General of the Sisters of Mercy of this country informs me that she is writing you about sending one of her Sisters to your hospital for the purpose of getting a year's training in nursing.

I may say that the Mother General is writing to you at my suggestion. I have it in mind to establish, as soon as feasible, in this Diocese a Hospital under the control of the Sisters of Mercy. As the Sisters have had no Hospital up to the present time, we have no Sisters who are trained nurses.

---

1. Sr. M. Francis Hickey, *Mercy Communico*, RG 10/9/31, ASMSJ, 3. St. Clare's Home for Working Girls continued to function until 1922. During the time it was in operation, besides Sr. M. Pius Mulcahy and Sr. M. Bernard Gladney, Sr. M. Antonia Egan, Sr. M. Ita Glynn, and Sr. Margaret Mary St. John held the office of superior.

If, as I hope, I shall be able to make a beginning within a year or two, I am desirous of having at least one of our Sisters familiar with hospital work who would be able to take charge of the Institution; and it is with a view to getting an insight into hospital work generally and some training in nursing that I suggested to the Mother General to send one of her Sisters to some hospital under the charge of the Sisters of Mercy.[2]

Eventually, in August 1918, Sr. M. Bernard Gladney set off for Pittsburgh to begin a three-year course in nursing, thus taking the first step in what was to become—if not a new ministry for the Sisters of Mercy of Newfoundland—one that was highly organized and in an institutional setting.[3] It will be noticed that in his letter the archbishop suggested "a year's training." The far-sighted and highly intelligent Sr. M. Bridget O'Connor would have none of this! If her congregation was to be responsible for a hospital, nothing but the best and most complete training available at the time would do. And so, Sr. M. Bernard Gladney, and those who followed her, completed not only the regular courses required to earn the certificate as a registered nurse, but they also took additional courses that would qualify them to perform specialized medical procedures.[4]

Two years later, in the summer of 1920, Sr. M. Bernard returned to St. John's for a short vacation. When she sailed for Pittsburgh a few weeks later to complete her training, she was

---

2. Archbishop E. P. Roche to Sister Superior, Mercy Hospital, Pittsburgh, PA, August 9, 1918, AASJ.

3. It will be remembered from earlier chapters that the care of the sick had always been an important part of the ministry of the Sisters of Mercy.

4. Sr. M. Bridget O'Connor's policy to ensure that sisters who nursed at St. Clare's were as highly qualified as possible was carried on by her successors. A glance at the degrees and specialties obtained by the Sisters of Mercy who nursed at St. Clare's is most impressive by any standard of medical excellence.

accompanied by Sr. M. Aloysius Rawlins, who had expressed an interest in studying dietetics and office management. However, Sr. M. Bridget O'Connor, who was never afraid of taking a risk, this time decided to err on the side of caution. She suggested to the talented Sr. M. Aloysius that, in addition to the courses she had already selected, she pursue studies in vocal and instrumental music at Mount Mercy, which was also in Pittsburgh, just in case the archbishop's plans for St. Clare's Mercy Hospital did not materialize! [5]

On October 21, 1921, Sr. M. Bernard Gladney returned to St. John's as a registered nurse. In addition to the regular program of studies, she had completed special courses in radiography, anaesthesia, and a medical students' laboratory course. Immediately on her return, she was appointed superior of St. Clare's Home, which continued to operate without interruption for the next six months.[6] Nevertheless, by this time, the plans for converting the home into a hospital had been finalized.

Early in May 1922, St. Clare's Home closed its doors. As soon as the last resident moved out, an army of carpenters, painters, plumbers, and electricians moved in. The men worked all day and through the night in their efforts to adapt St. Clare's Home to a twenty-bed hospital. It was a tribute to their skill and perseverance that in three weeks the hospital was ready to receive the first patient.

On May 21, 1922, Mass was celebrated by Archbishop Roche in the temporary chapel and St. Clare's Mercy Hospital was declared officially open. In his address, the archbishop noted that care of the sick is one of the most important ministries of the Sisters of Mercy, and he voiced his hopes for the future growth of the institution:

---

5. Sr. M. Aloysius Rawlins, besides other accomplishments, was a well-trained and gifted musician.

6. Hickey, *Mercy Communico*, RG 10/9/31, ASMSJ, 3.

We feel that this work, so eminently in harmony with the spirit of their Order will grow and prosper. They are beginning in a very humble way, a philanthropic work which has vast possibilities for good; they are planting a tiny grain of mustard seed, which we hope will grow into an immense tree, throwing its healing branches over different sections of the country.[7]

The archbishop could not have seen that before fifty years had passed, the little hospital in the "White House" would grow into a huge 375-bed institution with a staff of health care professionals numbering in the hundreds and operating on a budget totalling millions of dollars. Neither could the Presentation Sister, M. Clare English, have envisioned that her dream of a hostel for working girls would, in God's plan, become a place of healing and hope for thousands of Newfoundlanders.

---

7. Archbishop E. P. Roche, Address given at the opening of St. Clare's Mercy Hospital, St. John's, May 21, 1922, quoted in Hennebury, "St. Clare's," ASMSJ, 5.

TRIALS AND TRIBULATIONS

The marvellous richness of human experience would lose something of rewarding joy if there were no obstacles to overcome. The hilltop hour would not be half so wonderful if there were no dark valleys to traverse.

—Helen Keller

On the morning of May 22, 1922, the day after the official dedication of St. Clare's Mercy Hospital, Sr. M. Bernard Gladney woke up to a whole new set of challenges. She had been the superior of St. Clare's Home up to the time it closed, and now she was superior of St. Clare's Convent and administrator of St. Clare's Mercy Hospital. As she surveyed her small staff, she must have experienced no small degree of trepidation. She had assumed a heavy responsibility, but on the other hand, she was a woman of great inner strength and courage. She was assisted by a young registered nurse, Alice Casey, RN;[1] Miss Gladys Healey; and two Sisters of Mercy, Sr. M. Gabriel Fleming and Sr. M. Catherine Greene.[2] The first members of the medical staff were Dr.

---

1. Alice Casey was a native of Harbour Grace, Newfoundland, and a graduate of the school of nursing at the General Hospital in St. John's. She married John Higgins, a prominent St. John's lawyer. Her younger sister, Carmel Casey, followed her example in choosing nursing as a career. Carmel Casey, too, was associated with St. Clare's Mercy Hospital for a number of years.

2. Other Sisters of Mercy who assisted the registered nurses in the early days of St. Clare's were Sr. Margaret Mary St. John, Sr. M. Ignatius Molloy, and Sr. M. Agnes Doyle.

John Murphy, Dr. Andrew Carnell, Dr. James Grieve, Dr. F. W. Burden, Dr. Cluny Macpherson,[3] Dr. J. Scully, Dr. J. Fallon, Dr. J. B. O'Reilly, Dr. Hunter Cowperthwaite, Dr. Thomas Anderson, Dr. T. M. Mitchell, and Dr. N. S. Fraser.

In light of the origin of St. Clare's, it was appropriate that the first patient to be admitted to St. Clare's Mercy Hospital was a Presentation Sister, M. Benedict MacKenzie. Sr. M. Benedict was greeted with open arms and treated with tender care until she was well enough to return home fully cured. The first surgery performed in the new hospital was a thyroidectomy by Dr. N. S. Fraser.[4] The first baby to be born at St. Clare's was Arthur Morris who, more than twenty years later, graduated from medical school and practised in St. John's for many years as a successful physician. The first baby girl to be born at St. Clare's was Margaret Armstrong Kearney. The new St. Clare's Mercy Hospital was on its way and the future looked bright.

The little hospital soon gained a superb reputation for its care of the sick, and within a short time, it was functioning at full capacity. Then, just over a year later, disaster struck when the administrator, Sr. M. Bernard Gladney, contracted tuberculosis. Immediately, the superior general of the Sisters of Mercy, Sr. M. Bridget O'Connor, made arrangements for Sr. M. Bernard to go to the Saranac Sanatorium in New York for rest and treatment. An attempt was made to secure a qualified nurse from one of the other hospitals in St. John's to take over the responsibilities of the twenty-bed hospital until two other Sisters of Mercy had

---

3. Dr. Cluny Macpherson was the inventor of the world's first gas mask. It became the first gas mask to be used by the British army. This Newfoundlander's invention was the most important protective device of the First World War, shielding countless soldiers from blindness, disfigurement, or injury to their throats and lungs. Gas masks are worn by millions of soldiers around the world today.
4. Hennebury, "St. Clare's," ASMSJ, 6.

completed the necessary training, but to no avail.[5] None of the sisters who had been helping the two registered nurses at the hospital had formal training and the young Alice Casey was reluctant to take on the responsibility alone. The disappointed archbishop agreed to suspend admission to the hospital while the superior general, Sr. M. Bridget O'Connor, and her council looked to the Sisters of Mercy in the United States for help.

As the first step in her campaign to secure a nursing staff for the hospital, Sr. M. Bridget sent Sr. M. Consilio Kenny to visit the Sisters of Mercy of Philadelphia to inquire if that community would be willing to release a nurse until two Newfoundland sisters could be trained as nurses. The Philadelphia sisters, however, had no sister-nurse to spare. It should be noted here that Sr. M. Consilio was not only a persistent person, but also a very wise woman. If there was no help to be obtained from Philadelphia, Sr. M. Consilio was prepared to canvas every Mercy hospital in the United States—and beyond, if necessary. And so, she decided to try Mercy Hospital in Baltimore, Maryland. This time, instead of going directly to the sisters, she arranged an appointment with Archbishop Michael J. Curley of Baltimore and explained to him the plight of St. Clare's and the purpose of her visit to the United States. The archbishop was sympathetic to her request and, armed with his approval and support, Sr. M. Consilio set out for Mercy Hospital. The sisters there received her with great kindness and, acting on Archbishop Curley's suggestion, agreed to send Sr. M. Carmelita Hartman, the superior of the Mount Washington community of the Sisters of Mercy in Maryland, and Sr. M. Teresita McNamee, a registered nurse from Mercy Hospital in Baltimore, to St. John's to assess the situation.

Sr. M. Carmelita Hartman had held several important positions in different convents in Baltimore and, at the time

---

5. Ibid.

she came to Newfoundland, was the superior of the convent at Mercy Hospital in that city. Subsequently, when most of the Mercy convents in the United States were brought under one general administration, Sr. M. Carmelita was elected as the first superior general of the Sisters of Mercy of the Union.[6]

Sr. M. Teresita McNamee was an experienced nurse who was used to dealing with difficult and unusual situations. Toward the end of the First World War, an epidemic of Spanish Influenza broke out at the military base at Camp Meade, Maryland. Because of the severity of the outbreak and the few nurses available to care for the sick, the army asked for volunteers. Immediately, Sr. M. Teresita McNamee volunteered for duty at the base hospital. She remained there until the epidemic had run its course.[7]

These were the two Sisters of Mercy who came to Newfoundland to offer their help at a time of crisis at the new St. Clare's Mercy Hospital. As soon as the staff at St. Clare's heard of the impending arrival of the sisters from Baltimore, they went into action. The hospital was scrubbed from top to bottom, the beds made, and the equipment inspected and prepared for use. Upon their arrival, on October 24, 1923,[8] the two sisters from the United States participated enthusiastically in these activities. Sr. M. Teresita McNamee supervised all aspects of the preparations for reopening the medical and surgical wards, while Sr. M. Carmelita Hartman assumed the duty of "chief cook and bottle-washer" as she prepared meals, answered the phone and door bell, and bought supplies for various hospital departments. Within a matter of days after the arrival of the two American sisters, the hospital was ready for the reception of patients.

At the reopening of St. Clare's Mercy Hospital, Sr. M.

6. Archives of the Sisters of Mercy, Baltimore, MD. The author is indebted to Sr. M. Paula Marlin, RSM, of Baltimore for this information.

7. Ibid.

8. *Inter Nos* 1, no. 3 (February 1924), RG 10/9/84, ASMSJ, 50.

Aloysius Rawlins was appointed superior of the convent and administrator of the hospital and Sr. M. Teresita McNamee, director of nursing service. To complete the professional staff, the hospital hired several young graduates from the St. John's General Hospital Training School. Many years later, the sisters who lived at St. Clare's in those early days told stories of the joys and difficulties encountered in nursing the sick in a hospital that was still in its infancy. Much depended on the natural ability and inherited knowledge of the sisters who worked beside the few registered nurses on the staff. Nevertheless, these sisters were by no means unskilled novices in looking after the sick. Aside from on-the-job training they had received from Sr. M. Bernard Gladney, most of them had grown up in outport Newfoundland where there was no doctor available and people depended on the women of the settlement to care for their sick. A great deal of medical folklore had been passed down from generation to generation, and in addition, many young girls were accustomed to helping their mother look after sick and elderly relatives. Writing of this period in the history of St. Clare's, Sr. M. Fabian Hennebury noted:

> If the methods used for sterilizing the instruments in the Operating Room and for conveying patients back to bed following Surgery are difficult for us to envisage, the Sisters had an efficiency born of knowledge, skill, and necessity. They knew what improvising meant.[9]

Some of the improvisations would cause raised eyebrows in these days of modern technology and sophisticated equipment. For instance, methods of sterilization might fall far short of what might be considered essential today. The sisters and nurses at St. Clare's in the early 1920s depended on the efficacy of boiling water and vigorous scrubbing to ensure that no trace of contagion

9. Hennebury, "St. Clare's," ASMSJ, 7.

remained on instruments or other materials used in treating patients. So well did they boil and scrub that the records show that nobody picked up an infection as a result of being in St. Clare's. The wheeled, cushioned, and many-gadgeted stretchers of today's hospitals were unheard of in those days. Patients at St. Clare's who could not walk were transported in one of two ways, in a blanket or—when necessary—on a board well padded with folded blankets. On the maternity floor, when infants arrived in greater numbers than had been anticipated, makeshift bassinets were constructed of Carnation Milk cartons, well lined with the softest of warm, woolly blankets.[10] Undoubtedly, these hastily improvised cots, crafted by loving hands, provided their tiny occupants with just as much warmth and comfort as the professional bassinets supplied by some impersonal manufacturing company in Montreal. In any case, judging by repeated visits to the maternity ward, mothers seemed to be quite content with the accommodations provided for their offspring. Sometimes, however, an impatient baby would decide to arrive ahead of time. If this happened when all the maternity beds were occupied, a sister would give up her own bed to the new mother.[11] The sister, thus deprived, would most likely spend the night in a comfortable chair in the reception room of the hospital—for in those days, the chairs in convents were not designed for comfort.

While Sr. M. Teresita McNamee and her staff were attending to the needs of the sick, the General Council of the Sisters of Mercy was making plans to ensure that there would

---

10. The author is indebted to Sr. M. Fabian Hennebury for this information. When she was a very young probationer, if the number of babies exceeded the number of bassinets available, it was Sr. M. Fabian's duty to look for suitable cartons and prepare them to receive these little persons who had just made an entrance into this world.

11. Sr. M. Loretta McIsaac, quoted by Sr. M. Fabian Hennebury in an address given at the annual general meeting of St. Clare's Alumnae, 1992, MG 31/2/2, ASMSJ. The sisters' sleeping quarters were on the third floor, the attic of the hospital.

be a sufficient number of local sisters trained as nurses to carry on the work of the hospital. Already, in 1923, Sr. M. Joseph Byrne and Sr. M. Stanislaus Parsons had begun a program of nursing studies that would be completed in 1926. However, by that time, Sr. M. Teresita McNamee, having given two years of service to St. Clare's Mercy Hospital, had returned to Baltimore. Archbishop Roche and the Mercy Sisters in Newfoundland were well aware of the generosity of the Mercy Sisters in Baltimore in allowing one of their most capable and knowledgeable nurses to remain for such a long period of time. And so, when Sr. M. Teresita returned to Baltimore early in 1925, she took with her the undying gratitude of the Congregation of the Sisters of Mercy of Newfoundland.

In 1947, St. Clare's Mercy Hospital printed a special booklet to commemorate the silver jubilee of the founding of the hospital. In this booklet, the Newfoundland congregation of the Sisters of Mercy expressed gratitude to the American Sisters as follows:

> The History of St. Clare's would certainly be incomplete without a grateful tribute to the Sisters of Mercy of the Province of Maryland, U.S.A., who, in the early years of the Hospital, so generously gave the services of one of their most efficient nurses during the period of training of our own Sisters. Mother Mary Carmelita, the first Superior General of the American Sisters of Mercy, and her esteemed community have preserved throughout the years the deepest interest in everything connected with St. Clare's. A bond of friendship has been formed between the two Communities which, we pray may continue as time goes on.[12]

---

12. St. Clare's Mercy Hospital, *St. Clare's Mercy Hospital*, 1922–1947, Silver Jubilee Booklet (St. John's: n.p., 1947), 4.

NEW BEGINNINGS

Take the first step in faith.
You don't have to see the whole staircase, just take the first step.

—Martin Luther King, Jr.

The departure of Sr. M. Teresita McNamee might have left St. Clare's once more without a competent director of nursing services except that a young Newfoundlander, Marcella O'Connor, had recently graduated from St. Vincent's Hospital in New York. When she returned to St. John's early in 1925, she was offered the position of director of nursing services at St. Clare's, just in time to take over that position from Sr. M. Teresita McNamee. Marcella O'Connor held this position until September of 1926, when Sr. M. Joseph Byrne and Sr. M. Stanislaus Parsons returned home as fully qualified registered nurses. According to the plan of the General Council of the Sisters of Mercy, the return of the two sisters from Baltimore signalled the departure of another two to begin training at Mercy Hospital, Sr. M. Magdalen Baker and Sr. M. Loretta McIsaac. Both sisters had worked at St. Clare's after their profession and, for each, the experience had confirmed her desire to pursue a career in nursing. Sr. M. Loretta and Sr. M. Magdalen sailed for Baltimore early in September 1926. Both sisters were young, intelligent, and eager to make the most of the opportunities offered them. They worked long hours in the hospital, and in their free time, they pored over books, wanting to extract every ounce of knowledge that would help them in their profession. Before returning to Newfoundland in 1929, they had not only concluded their studies at Mercy Hospital in Baltimore and qualified as registered nurses, but they had also completed post-graduate training at Mary Immaculate Hospital in New York—Sr. M. Magdalen Baker in radiology and Sr. M. Loretta McIsaac in anaesthesia.[1]

On her return to St. Clare's Mercy Hospital in 1929, Sr. M. Loretta was appointed anaesthetist and supervisor of the operating room. She was also part-time supervisor of surgical patients. After the new St. Clare's was opened in 1939, she continued her duties in the operating room and, as well, took on the responsibility as supervisor of an eighteen-bed surgical unit. She retained these positions until 1949, when Newfoundland joined Canada. Then, because Canada did not recognize nurse anaesthetists, Sr. M. Loretta's long association with this branch of medicine came to an end—one of the casualties of Confederation with Canada! It must be recorded, however, that in all her years as anaesthetist, not one of Sr. M. Loretta's patients died as a result of an anaesthetic. Prevented by law from using her considerable training and experience in this field, Sr. M. Loretta was not willing to give up working in the hospital. She was appointed supervisor of central supply where her knowledge of the requirements of surgical and laboratory procedures was an invaluable asset. Then, when she finally retired in 1972, she continued her service to St. Clare's by volunteering at the information desk.

Sr. M. Loretta McIsaac was a woman who inspired a great deal of awe in those who saw her only in her role as a professional nurse. Because so many of her years were spent in the operating room, most people who came under her care remember her only for the few moments when she urged, "Take a deep breath." Sr. M. Loretta was a brisk, no-nonsense

---

1. Hennebury, "St. Clare's," ASMSJ, 8.

woman whose approach to life was intelligent, direct, and totally compassionate.[2]

When Sr. M. Magdalen Baker returned to St. Clare's, she worked as a supervisor of patient units. Then, when the radiology department opened in 1939, she was appointed supervisor of the department.[3] She was, in fact, the first registered X-ray technologist in Newfoundland and a founding member of the Society of Radiological Technologists. She reigned supreme over the X-ray department of St. Clare's for more than forty years and shared the experience she had gained over these years with many young X-ray technicians who owe much of their skill and knowledge to her instruction and guidance.[4]

The return of Sr. M. Loretta McIsaac and Sr. M. Magdalen Baker to St. Clare's in 1929 signalled the departure of the next pair of sisters to travel to Baltimore Mercy Hospital, Sr. M. St. Joan McDonnell[5] and Sr. M. Aloysius Rawlins. Their graduation in 1935 made a total of seven Newfoundland Sisters of Mercy who had completed the required studies and qualified as registered nurses in the United States. But there was still one more.

Shortly after Sr. M. Aloysius Rawlins and Sr. M. St. Joan McDonnell arrived at Mercy Hospital School of Nursing, they discovered there another young Newfoundlander by the name

2. On June 27, 1976, Sr. M. Loretta McIsaac completed her volunteer service in the hospital as usual. Shortly after returning to the convent, she became ill and died within a few minutes.

3. In addition to supervising the radiology department, Sr. M. Magdalen Baker was supervisor of pediatrics for a few years.

4. After her retirement in 1972, Sr. M. Magdalen remained at St. Clare's until ill health required that she move to the nursing unit at St. Catherine's Convent, where she died in 1985.

5. Sr. M. St. Joan McDonnell was born in Salmonier, St. Mary's Bay. She was a graduate of St. Bride's College, Littledale, where she was accepted as a postulant for the Mercy congregation in 1919. After her profession in 1922, she taught in the convent schools in St. George's, Burin, and Bell Island, and in Our Lady of Mercy in St. John's before she began her nursing studies.

of Catherine Kenny. The two Sisters of Mercy were delighted to meet someone from home, a bright, vivacious young woman who regaled them with stories of her escapades during the few holidays permitted to student nurses of those days. Catherine's joyous approach to life and her delight in parties and entertainments of all kinds would have deceived someone less observant than Sr. M. Aloysius Rawlins. Sr. M. Aloysius saw in this apparently scatterbrained youngster a woman of steely determination and one who would not be easily discouraged from pursuing any objective she had set for herself. Also, to her surprise, Sr. M. Aloysius noticed that Catherine was present at daily Mass, even on mornings after she had worked a twelve-hour shift on night duty. Sr. M. Aloysius wondered if perhaps this young woman was searching for something deeper than her experiences of the social life of Baltimore. Eventually, Catherine Kenny approached Sr. M. Aloysius to ask for advice on how to become a member of the Congregation of the Sisters of Mercy of Newfoundland. Not surprised by this announcement, Sr. M. Aloysius went into action. She wrote to Sr. M. Philippa Hanley, the superior general in St. John's, and in short order, arrangements were made for Catherine Kenny to become a member of the Mercy congregation. Shortly after her return to Newfoundland, Catherine was admitted as a postulant at Littledale where, on her reception as a novice, she was given the name, Sr. Mary Xaverius. She worked as staff nurse at Littledale for a few years before being appointed to the nursing staff at St. Clare's. Her first appointment at the hospital was as a scrub nurse in the operating room. After "scrubbing" for a period of time, Sr. M. Xaverius Kenny assumed the position of supervisor in the nursing units of the hospital.

A number of sister-nurses at St. Clare's Mercy Hospital remained there all their lives; others moved to different convents in the congregation to provide nursing care for a few years before returning to St. Clare's. Sr. M. Joseph Byrne served as staff nurse at St. Bride's College, Littledale, and at St. Michael's Orphanage, Belvedere. In 1937, Sr. M. Aloysius Rawlins was reappointed as administrator of the hospital, a position she held until her death in 1951.[6] Sr. M. St. Joan McDonnell held several positions in the hospital—director of nursing services, director of the school of nursing, and day supervisor. Later, she was appointed administrator of St. Patrick's Mercy Home, a position she filled for six years. Sr. M. Stanislaus Parsons was the first director of the school of nursing at St. Clare's. Later she was elected superior general of the Sisters of Mercy of Newfoundland, and she also served a term as superior of St. Michael's Convent, Belvedere. These eight women were the pioneers of St. Clare's Mercy Hospital.[7] Few in numbers and working in less than ideal conditions, they laid the foundation and they lived to see St. Clare's become one of the principal health care facilities in Newfoundland. More than that, they established a philosophy of care whereby the sisters and their co-workers at St. Clare's "endeavoured to transform medical science in its complex organization into love and healing, generously and freely given." [8]

Because the building that housed the first St. Clare's had originally been a family home, and then a "home away from home" for young women, it seemed to retain that warm, cosy atmosphere of "home," even after it became a hospital. Rules for visiting hours—and for visitors—were observed, although exceptions were made as is seen by the following story that appeared in the *Evening Telegram* signed by a person who called himself "Veritas":

---

6. It will be remembered that Sr. M. Aloysius succeeded Sr. M. Bernard Gladney as administrator of St. Clare's in 1923, a position she held until 1931, when she went to the United States to qualify as a registered nurse.

7. Sr. M. Bernard Gladney, Sr. M. Joseph Byrne, Sr. M. Stanislaus Parsons, Sr. M. Loretta McIsaac, Sr. M. Magdalen Baker, Sr. M. Aloysius Rawlins, Sr. M. St. Joan McDonnell, and Sr. M. Xaverius (Catherine) Kenny.

8. Hennebury, "St. Clare's," ASMSJ, 1.

My parents, my younger brother and I lived on Hamilton Street . . . My brother and I were of pre-school age. One day my father told us that our mother had been rushed to the hospital, the evening before, and having given us our breakfast and washed and clothed us, he sent us out to play . . . We wandered . . . to the junction of Patrick Street and LeMarchant Road, where a clear cool spring bubbled out to the ground at the side of the road right behind where the memorial to Alcock and Brown now stands. We slaked our thirst there . . . Suddenly I caught sight of St. Clare's. Turning to my brother I said, "That's where Mom is; let's go in and see her," and without further ado we went to the door and entered, with myself in the lead. On entering we were confronted by two Sisters of Mercy. On enquiring our business and learning of our mission, one sister turned and smiled at the other, and taking us by the hand, led us through divers [sic] corridors into a room and to the bedside of our mother who was amazed and shocked at seeing a Sister appear at her bedside leading two small and somewhat grubby children, as it was not during visiting hours, and if it had been, children of our age would not have been allowed in anyway.[9]

Apparently, the sisters were willing to bend the rules in the case of a couple of small boys who missed their mother.

Within a few years, other young sisters chose nursing as a career and began their training at St. Clare's where, under the guidance of these first sister-nurses, they discovered much more than the science contained in the medical texts that they studied so assiduously. They were taught that the powerful concern of Jesus for the whole person was to be their guide. As nurses and as Sisters of Mercy, they learned

---

9. Veritas [pseud.], "Golden Jubilee of St. Clare's Home," Letters to the Editor, *Evening Telegram*, October 2, 1963, 6.

that their vocation was "to bring physical, spiritual and social health to God's creation and to enrich life wherever their ministry called them." [10]

As a private hospital, St. Clare's Mercy Hospital had no government funding. The hospital was intended to care for patients who were in a position to pay for hospital treatment. When a small extension was planned in 1929, the *Daily News* commented:

> St. Clare's, though small, is thoroughly and modernly equipped, and having regard to its size, has all the appointments that make for efficiency in hospital treatment, and that can conduce to the comfort of the patients. It is competently staffed, with two trained Nursing Sisters, Registered Nurses under the Maryland State Board; A Sister Dietician, trained at Mercy Hospital, Pittsburgh, two lay graduate nurses, and probationers. Two other Sisters have just graduated at the Mercy Hospital, Baltimore, and will be attached to the staff of St. Clare's in September. The hospital . . . is intended to provide accommodation for patients in a position to pay for hospital treatment, but from the beginning it has been an absolutely open hospital—open to all denominations and all members of the medical profession. The hospital is not privately endowed, nor does it receive a government grant, but is altogether financed by the fees from its patients. [11]

The sister-dietician, to whom this article referred, was the multi-talented Sr. M. Aloysius Rawlins, who was, at the same time, superior of the convent and business administrator of the hospital.

The 1929 extension to St. Clare's was of very modest

---

10. Hennebury, "St. Clare's," ASMSJ, 1.

11. *Daily News*, May 25, 1929, quoted in Hennebury, "St. Clare's," ASMSJ, 10.

dimensions. It was intended to meet in a small way the increasing demand by patients for accommodation. However, all that could be managed at the time was the addition of three or four extra private rooms and much-needed additional space for members of the staff. By September 1929, work on the extension had been completed.

In spite of the fact that St. Clare's received no help from government grants, it sometimes happened that the hospital was asked to admit urgent cases when there was no space available at the General Hospital. The *Daily News* pointed out that St. Clare's accepted government-subsidized patients at the rate of three dollars per day, with an extra operating fee for surgical cases. These rates covered all expenses— board, medicine, drugs, and surgical and medical supplies and attendance. Needless to say, the fee charged these patients was insufficient to cover only the actual cost of treatment. The *Daily News* continued:

> It would be impossible . . . to accept patients at these low rates but for the fact that the Sisters, whose life work it is, receive no remuneration for their services, and also for the further fact that the members of the medical profession generously give their medical and surgical services at reduced rates to patients paid for by the Department of Public Charities.[12]

It should be noted that the sisters at St. Clare's continued to work without remuneration until national health insurance was introduced in 1958.

From the period 1922–1939, other Sisters of Mercy who worked with the registered nurses at St. Clare's were: Sr. M. Ita Glynn, Sr. M. Bonaventure Reddy, Sr. M. Michael Gillis, Sr. M. Catherine Greene, Sr. M. Patricia Hogan, Sr. M. Gerard O'Reilly, Sr. M. Rose Power, and Sr. M. Dominica Flynn.

---

12. Ibid.

These sisters made the work of the nursing staff possible by serving as accountants, office personnel, and dietary personnel, and by supervising laundry, cleaning, and kitchen staffs. In fact, the ministry to the sick at St. Clare's could not have been carried on without them. Sr. M. Fabian Hennebury wrote of the nursing staff as follows:

> The six Nursing Sisters and a few probationary nurses who were given in-service clinical training, continued to care for the sick. The love and dedication with which they cared for their patients established in a short time a reputation for St. Clare's, and there was an increased demand for service.[13]

As the years passed, demands for admission to St. Clare's increased until, in 1937, the lack of space could no longer be ignored. On October 31, 1937, a letter from Archbishop Roche was read in all parishes of the archdiocese announcing his decision to build a new three-storey hospital. The task was regarded by many as utopian, since Newfoundland was in the midst of the worst depression in its history, and many influential people adamantly opposed the project.[14] Nevertheless, the people of the archdiocese and friends of all faiths generously responded to a drive for funds—so much so that approximately seventy-two thousand dollars was realized through parish collections and donations from individuals and businesses.[15] The Congregation of the Sisters of Mercy mortgaged the Littledale property and arranged a loan from the Eastern Trust

---

13. Hennebury, "St. Clare's," ASMSJ, 11.

14. Ibid.

15. For two years prior to the opening of the 1939 hospital, an annual collection was taken up on Easter Sunday in all churches of the archdiocese. After this practice ceased, some people continued to contribute anonymously to the support of the hospital. The author is indebted to Sr. M. Fabian Hennebury for this information.

Company.[16] In addition, Archbishop Roche asked that all other funds, money saved by the Mercy congregation over the years for emergencies, go toward the building of the hospital, "which is to all intents and purposes the property of the Mercy Order in Newfoundland."[17] The total cost of the building was approximately $300,000, a very large amount in those days.

On May 23, 1938, work began on the new hospital with the erection of offices and sheds, and on July 25, the first concrete was poured. A tin box containing medals, photographs, and a signed statement by the archbishop was placed in the first block of concrete.[18]

All along, the sisters had realized that the archbishop's plan for a three-floor institution would not be adequate to meet the demands for service. They realized, further, that it would take a strong lobby to persuade the archbishop to change his mind. They decided to pray to St. Jude, known as "the saint of impossible cases." Their novena finished on November 3, 1938, the day the exterior walls of the three-storey building were completed. As they sat down to lunch that day, the sisters acknowledged sadly that even St. Jude could not sway Archbishop Roche once he had determined on a course of action. But before they had finished their meal, the administrator of the hospital, Sr. M. Aloysius Rawlins, was called to the phone. She returned with the news that the archbishop had changed his mind and given instructions that an extra floor was to be added. This would result in a four-floor hospital. As well, many services could be carried out in the spacious basement area. Before they left the table, the sisters

16. St. Clare's Mercy Hospital, *St. Clare's Mercy Hospital, Historical Highlights, 1922–1972* (St. John's: n.p., 1972), ASMSJ, 1. In addition, the Congregation of the Sisters of Mercy provided a loan of $56,000 at 2½ percent interest.

17. Archbishop Roche to Sr. M. Bridget O'Connor, superior general of the Sisters of Mercy, August 12, 1938, ASMSJ.

18. According to Sr. M. Fabian Hennebury, the block containing these articles was placed at the centre of the rear of the building.

had made the unanimous decision to name the additional floor in honour of St. Jude, and for many years, the fourth floor of St. Clare's was known as St. Jude's Hall. Three weeks later, the roof was finished and a cross, electrically illuminated, was erected over the hospital. This cross shone out over St. John's and could be seen even far out at sea by sailors and fishermen. Spanish and Portuguese sailors who fell ill at sea and were brought to St. Clare's for treatment spoke of the comfort of seeing that cross shining through the darkness.

On October 29, 1939, sixteen months after construction began, the new hospital was blessed and formally opened. It was with a great deal of pride that Archbishop Roche, recalling the small beginnings of 1922, declared:

Today, after seventeen years, we are assembled in this splendid new Hospital to see the completion of the work which was then begun. We are opening a large modern Hospital, with accommodation for one hundred patients, built on the most approved scientific lines, equipped with everything that modern hospitalization requires, under the management of a staff that comprises eight trained Nursing Sisters, competent and experienced lay graduates, and a training school of some thirty nurses. Verily, my dear Sisters, the acorn has developed into a mighty oak; the tiny grain of mustard seed has grown, as we hoped it would into a mighty tree.[19]

There was general rejoicing over the opening of the modern, new hospital and widespread appreciation of the contribution of the Sisters of Mercy to the institution. Shortly after the hospital opened, the following article appeared in the *Monitor* under the caption, "Soul of the New St. Clare's":

---

19. Archbishop E. P. Roche, Address given at the opening of St. Clare's Mercy Hospital, St. John's, October 29, 1939, RG 10/9/62, ASMSJ.

Completed, equipped, and running at practically full capacity, St. Clare's Mercy Hospital is designed to play an important part in the life of the community, not only because it represents the best that modern architecture and hospital science can provide, but as well because it is staffed by the Sisters of Mercy, an Order whose work in this field is famed all over the American continent. The building is only the body, they are the soul. Indeed, in this city, they have established themselves as something more than merely capable, scientifically trained competent nurses, they bring to hospital administration more than efficiency. They bring an atmosphere created by their own consecrated lives of devotion to the sick and the suffering. It is this that makes the difference between a hospital and a Catholic hospital, and their presence is the surest guarantee of the fine services St. Clare's will render to Newfoundland.[20]

---

20. "Soul of the New St. Clare's," *The Monitor* 6, no. 12 (December 16, 1939), 10.

THE NEXT STEP

There will come a time when you believe everything is finished. That will be the beginning.

—Louis L'Amour

The decision by Archbishop Roche and the Sisters of Mercy to build the new hospital took a good deal of courage and trust in God's Providence, for it was made at a period in history that was filled with uncertainty.[1]

In his address at the official opening of the new hospital, the archbishop referred to the Second World War that had just begun. He noted:

The dark clouds of war are heavy over a great part of the world, and its shadows are falling dimly over us here in this country. We can, as it were, hear the thunder and noise of the battle, the clash of arms . . . How strangely it all contrasts with this quiet ceremony this morning, opening this haven of healing and rest, the atmosphere of which breathes, as I hope it ever will, "the peace of Christ in the kingdom of Christ."[2]

---

1. It should be mentioned that, coincidental with the opening of the new hospital, the Sisters of Mercy were planning the construction of an addition to Our Lady of Mercy School in St. John's. The new building, opened in 1942, was to commemorate the centenary of the arrival of the Sisters of Mercy in St. John's. The addition to the school consisted of an auditorium, a gymnasium, a dance studio, and several music rooms.

2. *The Monitor* 6, no. 10 (October 31, 1939), 9.

However, the war was still far away, and up to this point, Newfoundlanders had not experienced the pain and suffering of losing fathers, husbands, sons, and brothers who had gone overseas in service to their country.

During the first few weeks after its formal opening, St. Clare's was not without its share of distinguished visitors. In November, the governor of Newfoundland, Sir Humphrey Walwyn, and Lady Walwyn paid an official visit. Lady Walwyn presented the hospital with a picture of the Virgin Mary in a frame of hard wrought brass of ancient design. This had been in Lady Walwyn's family for over seventy years and was purchased in Italy in 1872 by her great-aunt, Lady van Strawbridge, wife of the governor of Malta at the time.[3]

The first patients were admitted to the new hospital on November 15, 1939. Nine of these were transferred from the "old" St. Clare's, the first of these being Mrs. D. J. Jackman of Bell Island. The first infant to be born in the new hospital arrived that very night—the daughter of Mr. and Mrs. Bruce Connolly of Craigmillar Avenue in St. John's.

Initially, due to lack of funds, the rooms of the hospital were very simply furnished. In fact, it was a few years before the white plastered walls were painted. This state of affairs was disturbing to the sister-nurses who, once they had returned to the seclusion of the convent, voiced daily complaints to the administrator, Sr. M. Aloysius Rawlins. And so, as soon as she could lay her hands on a few extra dollars, Sr. M. Aloysius saw to it that the private and semi-private rooms were furnished with standing lamps, easy chairs, and matching drapes and chair covers.

However, right from the beginning, the quality of the meals served to the patients was of primary concern to the staff

---

3. For many years, this picture hung in the boardroom of the hospital. It is now preserved in the Archives of the Sisters of Mercy, St. John's.

of St. Clare's. Food from the main kitchen was conveyed by dumb waiter to the kitchenette on each floor and served from a steam table. This table was attached to a gas burner for heating the water—the tea was always made "on the spot," and coffee was freshly perked. With this decentralized service, the meals were kept hot, and linen tray clothes and serviettes, china, and silverware were used on all trays. The responsibility for this service was added to the workload of the sister-supervisors, for the sisters considered a hot, tasty meal, served in an attractive manner, an essential factor in the recovery of the patient.[4]

Following the opening of the new hospital in 1939, the sisters and staff continued to work hard to provide a high standard of care. Sr. M. Fabian Hennebury remembered that they worked twelve hours a day—and sometimes more—seven days a week. In addition to the sisters, there were only five graduate nurses on staff, with a sister-supervisor on each floor. The duties of the supervisor included not only nursing care but also serving meals. While members of the lay staff were given a free afternoon once a week, the sisters continued to work as usual.[5]

During the period from 1922 through the 1940s the sisters, for the most part, were the only supervisors. Graduate nurses assisted them in the operating room, delivery room, pediatrics, and nursery. Sr. M. Joseph Byrne and Sr. M. Xaverius (Catherine) Kenny[6] rotated on night duty for periods which lasted initially from several months to a couple of years. However, as other sisters graduated, they were included in the

---

4. Hennebury, "St. Clare's," ASMSJ, 23.

5. Later, this free time for lay staff was increased to a full day off once a week.

6. In 1968–1969, the Sisters of Mercy in Newfoundland were given the option of returning to the use of their baptismal name or retaining their religious name. Sr. M. Xaverius Kenny chose to return to her baptismal name, Catherine.

rotation. This inclusion meant that the night supervisor worked from three- to six-month periods at a time.

It is doubtful that the sisters who lived in other convents realized or appreciated the almost ceaseless labour of the nursing sister at St. Clare's. Although there was a certain amount of visiting back and forth by sisters to neighbouring convents in the city, these visits rarely included St. Clare's Convent—not because sisters were not welcome at St. Clare's, but because work and recreation schedules of hospital and schools did not coincide. Thus, for some years, the overworked sisters at St. Clare's had only occasional social contacts with other members of their congregation. Furthermore, teaching sisters were frequently changed from one convent to another according to their qualifications and the needs of the schools in different parts of Newfoundland. Most sisters lived with dozens of different people in the span of ten to fifteen years. St. Clare's, however, was a more static community. The only changes occurred when sisters destined for the school of nursing came to live at St. Clare's Convent. This might have led to a feeling of isolation except that, having the good sense to realize that this is the way things were at the time, the St. Clare's sisters accepted their lot with good-humoured grace. Opportunities for them to forge closer bonds with other members of the congregation occurred during their two-week vacation or when a sister from another community required hospitalization. The joy with which the sister-nurses greeted the sister-patient often caused the poor sufferer to wonder at the peculiar attitude of St. Clare's sisters who, apparently, regarded the illness of another sister as an occasion for celebration! Nonetheless, there was no place in the rigid schedule of a nurse to permit her to spend much time at the bedside of another member of her congregation. Sr. M. Stanislaus Parsons, in particular, was adamant in insisting that the time of the nurse not be wasted in paying visits to her friends.

Because St. Clare's Mercy Hospital was completely self-supporting, there was a tight control on all spending and strict supervision of the supplies that were available. In her history of St. Clare's Mercy Hospital, Sr. M. Fabian Hennebury wrote:

> It was not unknown . . . for the student Nurses and others to bring in a supply of dresses and diapers from home for the Nursery and Pediatric Departments. Preparation of formulas was also a part of the nurses' daily routine . . . Bottles and nipples were boiled after each feeding. It was not uncommon to get the aroma of burnt up nipples, or see a student or orderly running to the nearby drugstore to purchase a replacement.[7]

Shortly after the new hospital opened in 1939, Archbishop Roche made one stipulation to the sisters—any mother who wanted to be admitted to St. Clare's to deliver her baby would not be refused because of inability to pay. This was a laudable sentiment, and one with which the Sisters of Mercy heartily agreed. The only hitch was that the sisters depended on the income from fees paid by the patients to support the hospital; provide equipment, supplies, food, heat, et cetera; and to pay the staff. As it was, they just managed to pay the bills and keep solvent. The archbishop understood this and decided to approach the government, knowing that other hospitals were reimbursed for the expenses involved in caring for those who could not afford to pay for themselves. His request was favourably received, and Dr. Leonard Miller, the medical officer for hospital admission, received the following directions from the secretary of Public Health and Welfare:

> Please note that effective immediately this Department has established the understated relations with the new St. Clare's Hospital.

---

7. Hennebury, "St. Clare's," ASMSJ, 26.

1. All poor maternity cases are to be sent to the St. Clare's Hospital where the patients are members of the Roman Catholic Church.

2. All pediatric cases are to be sent to this Institution, the rate of treatment quoted being less than that now charged at the Grace Hospital.

3. Emergency and other cases for which accommodation cannot be found at the General Hospital are to be sent to St. Clare's.[8]

According to the correspondence between St. Clare's and the Commission of Government, the hospital requested two dollars and fifty cents a day for maternity cases referred by the government; the charge for children of seven years of age and under was two dollars per day; and, in the case of other government patients, the hospital requested a daily rate of three dollars. It appears that the government objected to the three dollar rate. On November 28, 1939, in a letter to Sir John C. Puddester, commissioner for Public Health and Welfare, the archbishop agreed to lower the rate for government patients to two dollars and fifty cents a day—the rate charged at the General Hospital. His Grace added, "It is, of course, understood that operating room fee, X-ray, etc. will be, as heretofore, extra charges."[9] At the same time, the archbishop presented a petition for assistance for laundry services, but this time the government was not so accommodating and refused to provide any help.[10]

Even at 1939 prices, the amount paid by the government for indigent patients was not nearly enough to cover the cost of

---

8. H. M. Mosdell, MD, secretary of Public Health and Welfare, to Leonard Miller, MD, November 14, 1939, 107/24, AASJ.

9. Archbishop Roche to Sir John C. Puddester, November 28, 1939, 107/24, AASJ.

10. Puddester to Archbishop Roche, November 16, 1939, 107/24, AASJ.

care. Furthermore, the government reimbursed St. Clare's only for those patients who were referred because of religious affiliation. Thus, the hospital received no remuneration for young mothers who were referred to other hospitals but who applied to come to St. Clare's. Nevertheless, no young woman who sought admission to St. Clare's was refused because of inability to pay. The hospital struggled along until 1944, when the archbishop requested that St. Clare's receive a portion of the grant that the government provided to the Grace Hospital for the care of obstetrical patients.

> In 1944 a request was made to the Department of Health by Archbishop E. P. Roche, that a portion of the grant then paid to the Grace General Hospital for the care of obstetrical patients be given to St. Clare's for poor mothers who preferred to come to St. Clare's.[11]

The archbishop's request was denied.

With no further help from the government, the hospital had to rely on the ingenuity of the sisters at St. Clare's to come up with a solution to the problem of how to cover the costs involved in caring for these young mothers and their babies. In short order they came up with a brilliant idea—the creation of the "Burse." The superior of St. Clare's Convent at the time, Sr. M. Benedicta Fitzgibbon, wrote a letter to friends of St. Clare's to explain the sisters' plan and to elicit support:

> His Grace, the Archbishop . . . gave to the Sisters one special injunction that no maternity case was to be refused admission because of inability to pay. This desire of His Grace had been faithfully carried out even in the case of mothers presenting,

---

11. Hennebury, "Appendix 4, Historical Summary of Financial Operation, St. Clare's Mercy Hospital (1922–1983)" in "St. Clare's," ASMSJ.

from the Department of Health, admission slips to other institutions. Acceptance of such cases has never been refused even though the Hospital must care for them without government remuneration. It will be seen, however, that such demands weigh heavily upon an institution dependent entirely on its income from private sources . . . These reasons impels us to begin in a small way the creation of a fund for this purpose . . . We are placing this project under the patronage of the powerful protector of the Holy Family, St. Joseph, naming the fund, "St. Joseph's Burse."[12]

The creation of St. Joseph's Burse met with an immediate response, and through the generosity of the benefactors of St. Clare's, hundreds of young mothers had the satisfaction of delivering their babies in the hospital of their choice. Many of these young women required more than ordinary care because they had not visited a doctor at any time during their pregnancy.

At that time, too, all Roman Catholic babies born at St. Clare's were baptized in the hospital chapel before their mothers were discharged. This was an especially joyous celebration. Proud parents, doting grandparents, and an assortment of fond relatives and friends assembled in St. Clare's chapel for the event. At the appointed time, the babies were carried in, each one attired in a long white garment adorned with the multiple frills and flounces characteristic of christening robes at that time. No infant was ever deprived of the luxury of a christening robe. If the mother could not afford one, it was provided by means of St. Joseph's Burse. After the ceremony was over and the wailing stars of the occasion were brought back to the nursery, the families celebrated with wine and a christening

---

12. Hennebury, "St. Clare's," ASMSJ, 32–33. From St. Joseph's Burse, the attendant physician was given a fee of twenty-five dollars for delivery and care, and the hospital was paid the munificent sum of two dollars and fifty cents a day.

cake. St. Joseph's Burse was discontinued in 1958 when the National Health Insurance Program was available to all citizens in Canada. Until that time, St. Clare's Mercy Hospital continued the practice of providing free accommodation and care to pregnant mothers who could not afford to pay a fee.

In addition to providing care to Newfoundlanders, St. Clare's also cared for seamen from many other countries, especially those from the Spanish and Portuguese fishing fleets. This was because two physicians who worked mainly at St. Clare's were also doctors employed by the Port of St. John's. During the Second World War, St. Clare's admitted many sailors from ships that had been torpedoed off the coast of Newfoundland. On one occasion, eleven seamen were admitted with severe frostbite, having been in lifeboats for several days before they were rescued. At the time of this occurrence, the hospital was working at peak capacity. In order to provide the special treatment that was needed, the office and the doctors' lounge were speedily transformed into nursing units to care for the injured sailors.[13]

In 1948, a new building containing the boiler room and laundry was constructed. This was connected by a tunnel to the main building. The cost of this new addition was $186,149. Once more, the Sisters of Mercy risked everything to finance this necessary addition to the hospital. A bond issue of $100,000 at 4 percent interest was established.[14] Sisters of Mercy in every convent in Newfoundland felt the pinch; however, they were used to a frugal lifestyle and accustomed to tightening their belts for the sake of the ministry of the congregation. It speaks well for the fiscal prudence and wise management of those women who directed the affairs of the Congregation of the Sisters of Mercy, as well as of the administrators of St. Clare's, that these loans were paid in full by 1968 without any outside assistance.

---

13. Hennebury, "St. Clare's," ASMSJ, 27.
14. Ibid., 18.

However, in spite of their delight in the new hospital that boasted the most up-to-date equipment available at the time, the sisters felt keenly the lack of a chapel—something that they considered to be an integral part of a Catholic hospital. It is true that there was a small room set aside in the hospital where visitors and patients could go to pray, but the need of a larger space was becoming more obvious by the day.

In 1947, on the occasion of Archbishop Roche's golden anniversary of ordination to the priesthood, the people of the archdiocese presented him with a gift of $83,000. The archbishop, for whom the welfare of St. Clare's was a priority, donated the entire amount toward the completion of a new chapel for St. Clare's. The chapel extension, on the west side of the 1939 building, also contained a new dining room and cafeteria, a twenty-eight bed pediatric unit, and an extension to the obstetrics department. This left more space for a large nursery and for patients on the first floor of the hospital. The total cost of the new wing was $235,000. In addition to the archbishop's donation, money was raised through bonds and bank loans. St. Clare's Convent contributed a further $54,000 from a savings account called the "Chapel Account." The money in this account was accumulated over the years from gifts from relatives and friends to individual sisters, as well as from special projects.[15]

The first Mass in the new chapel was celebrated by Archbishop Roche on March 19, 1950. This was the last time the ailing archbishop celebrated Mass publicly. During the summer of 1950, his health failed rapidly and in the middle of August, he was admitted to St. Clare's. He spent the last few weeks of his life in a suite that had been prepared for him on the second floor of the "White House"—the first St.

---

15. Because of their vow of poverty, the Sisters of Mercy were not permitted to retain for their personal use any monetary gifts they received. The gifts were deposited in the convent account, to be used in ministry projects or to assist the poor.

Clare's Mercy Hospital, which he had established in 1922.[16] Archbishop Roche died on September 23, 1950.

With the chapel extension in 1950, the capacity of the hospital was increased to one hundred and thirty-two beds. The dietary department, X-ray department, operating rooms, and other service areas originally planned for an eighty-bed hospital would have been totally inadequate were it not for the loyalty and hard work of the medical, nursing, and support personnel. Their dedication ensured that the high standard of patient care that had always been maintained at St. Clare's was not compromised by the increased capacity of the hospital. Also, the fact that during the period of 1939 to 1950 an additional nine Sisters of Mercy had received certification as registered nurses and the school of nursing had been established did much to relieve the burden carried by the seven sister-nurses who had borne the responsibility of the hospital since the early days.

16. The "White House" is now St. Clare's Mercy Convent.

St. Clare's Mercy Hospital School of Nursing[1]

Misericordia Super Omnia—Mercy Above All
—Motto of St. Clare's Mercy Hospital School of Nursing

From the very start of negotiations with Archbishop Roche to open St. Clare's Mercy Hospital, the superior general of the Sisters of Mercy, Sr. M. Bridget O'Connor, had her eye on the important matter of training enough nurses to operate the hospital efficiently. She realized that it would be necessary to offer some kind of educational program whereby young persons could come to St. Clare's and study nursing under the guidance of the sister-nurses.

Shortly after the hospital opened in 1922, several young ladies became students at the hospital under the supervision of Sr. M. Bernard Gladney. When Sr. M. Teresita McNamee replaced Sr. M. Bernard at the hospital in 1923, she organized daily classes and gave periodic examinations to evaluate performance. However, due to the small size of the hospital and inadequate teaching facilities it was not possible to issue diplomas. Nevertheless, these students had the rare advantage of a great deal of individual instruction and supervision. Students who showed an aptitude for nursing were encouraged by the sisters to move to other hospitals in

---

1. Although the history of St. Clare's Mercy Hospital School of Nursing is closely linked with the development and expansion of the hospital, it had its own identity. Thus, it seemed wise to treat the story of the school of nursing from its beginning to its closing in a separate chapter of this book.

Canada and the United States to continue their training and qualify as registered nurses.[2]

Coincidental with the opening of the new hospital in 1939 was the establishment of St. Clare's Mercy Hospital School of Nursing under the supervision of the first director of the school, Sr. M. Stanislaus Parsons. The school motto, "Misericordia Super Omnia (Mercy Above All)," was chosen by the archbishop and was to be the guiding principle of the hospital itself as well as of all St. Clare's graduates. Fourteen new nursing students moved into the new school of nursing and, at the same time, five young women who had begun their studies in the small 1922 hospital were transferred and were given advanced standing in some courses. These five young ladies were Lillian Coleman, Ethel Goff, Anne Hogan, Eileen O'Brien, and Margaret O'Reilly. They eventually became the first graduates of St. Clare's Mercy Hospital School of Nursing, receiving their diplomas at the first graduation ceremony held on February 19, 1941.

An important part of the plan to establish a school of nursing at St. Clare's was the matter of a residence for the students. The original students' residence, located on St. Clare Avenue, was comprised of two dwelling houses with two large dormitories and a few private and semi-private rooms. When viewed from the perspective of the twenty-first century, the quality of accommodation provided student nurses would appear to be totally inadequate. However, a graduate nurse from the class of 1949 remembered it quite differently:

> Whenever one thinks of those wonderfully happy years spent in training at St. Clare's . . . one's memory inevitably wanders back to those first and second years when we all shared

2. Sr. M. Calasanctius Power, "St. Clare's Mercy Hospital School of Nursing, 1939–1979," unpublished manuscript, ASMSJ, 1. Except where noted, the author is indebted to Sr. M. Calasanctius for most of the information on the school of nursing.

the upper and lower dormitories . . . We were like a family, almost as sisters, sharing our worries, our joys and all the concerns that went with being in training. The good times in the dorms had to come to a close when a new addition was added in 1948 [*sic*]. The new residence had a "nook" to replace our small social area, lots of bathrooms and even a fire escape. The students had private and semi-private rooms. It was nice to have improved accommodations but somehow we never had as much fun as we did in the dormitories.[3]

Night nurses were accommodated in separate dwelling houses—one on the corner of Springdale Street and Patrick Street, the other on LeMarchant Road. A modern, three-storey extension was added to the St. Clare Avenue residence in 1947. This eliminated the need for special accommodation for night nurses, and also provided extra social, lecture, and reception space.

The students' tuition, board, and laundry were furnished by the hospital. Because the hospital was entirely self-supporting, no stipend for students was possible until 1956. At that time, the administration of the hospital decided to increase patient ward rates in order to provide funds to allow students the princely stipend of twenty-five dollars per month. When, in July 1958, the hospital received financial assistance from the Government of Newfoundland, the stipend was increased to twenty-eight dollars a month.

In the early days of the school of nursing, social activities of the school provided outlets for varying tastes. Lively debates were in vogue, and something special was always created by the first year students for "Capping Day." Many St. Clare's graduates will recall the plays and the uproarious skits and parodies on different phases of nursing.

3. Catherine Kirby Burke, *Residence Recollections and Hospital Happenings* (St. John's: n.p., 1999), 4.

The years 1939–1945 were years of development and progress for St. Clare's Mercy Hospital School of Nursing. When Dr. J. B. Murphy addressed the nurses of the graduating class of 1945, he outlined the enormous progress made during the first six years of the hospital's school of nursing. When St. Clare's Mercy Hospital School of Nursing opened in 1939 with the extension of the small hospital, there was a supervising staff of seven registered nursing sisters in addition to the lay staff graduates. Within six years, a qualified anaesthetist, two X-ray technicians, a laboratory technician, a supervisor in pediatrics, a dietician, and an educational director had been added to the staff. This was in addition to lay employees and a sister-supervisor in each department. The increase in staff gives some idea of the growth in the development of both St. Clare's Mercy Hospital and St. Clare's Mercy Hospital School of Nursing.[4]

So that the program offered at St. Clare's would conform to accepted standards, Archbishop Roche made the following request in a letter to Sir John C. Puddester, commissioner for Public Health and Welfare:

The Sisters [at St. Clare's Mercy Hospital] are at present engaged in the Training School Department. Might I ask you to let me have the regulations of the Department with regard to training schools for nurses, as the Management is anxious to conform as closely as possible with your arrangements.[5]

From 1939 to 1958, formal classes were held in a classroom and an adjoining nursing arts room in the nurses' residence on St. Clare Avenue. The nursing program in the first ten years consisted of three full years of study. This included

---

4. "Graduation Class of the School of Nursing, St. Clare's Mercy Hospital, October 13th, 1945," *The Monitor* 11, no. 10 (October 1945), 1–3.

5. Archbishop Roche to Puddester, December 23, 1939, 107/24, AASJ.

a probationary period of five months, at the end of which the students received their cap and bib. This event marked their admission in the school of nursing as junior students. It was felt that with the probationary period completed, the most important part of instruction was now at the bedside. Hence, most of the students' learning experience came from being assigned to various services throughout the hospital. The sister-supervisor or head nurse was responsible for teaching and supervising the student. This was not always the best method, but it was the only one possible at the time.

Because there were no full-time instructors in the early years, some members of the medical staff offered their services as lecturers. Subjects taught by the doctors included anatomy, physiology, surgical and medical nursing, psychiatry, infectious diseases, pediatrics, obstetrics, and tuberculosis. In addition, religion and ethics were taught by priests from the archdiocese.

Students received individual attention in the operating room under the careful eye of the supervisor, Sr. M. Loretta McIsaac. Obstetrics was covered fully at St. Clare's in the third year of study under the discerning supervision of Sr. M. Fabian Hennebury and later, Sr. M. St. Clare Maddigan. Examinations were held and evaluated at the end of each course of study in the first, second, and third years, with the general standing of each student determined by her ability and adaptability as well as by her scholastic achievement. A pass mark of 60 percent was required in each subject. The Registered Nurses' Examinations were set and corrected by a committee of medical doctors through the Department of Health and under the control of the Newfoundland government until 1953, when, by an act of the provincial legislature, the Association of Registered Nurses of Newfoundland was inaugurated. Approval of the school of nursing program was granted by the Association of Registered Nurses of Newfoundland on May 22, 1957.[6]

6. Power, "St. Clare's," ASMSJ, 3.

During World War Two, because of the strategic position of St. John's, the city was in real danger of attack by the German submarines that prowled around the coast of Newfoundland. At night, the city was kept in total darkness and blackout rules were rigidly enforced. In addition to their nursing duties, student nurses were given the responsibility of seeing that, like all other buildings in the city, the hospital was thoroughly "blacked out." From sunset to dawn, large green blinds had to be drawn over all windows so that no light could be seen from outside the hospital.

In 1943, Sr. M. Xaverius Kenny was appointed director of the school of nursing, a post she held for thirty-one years. Relying largely on experience and natural ability, she administered the school of nursing in a manner that earned her the respect of visiting lecturers, colleagues, and, most of all, the students themselves. Despite her diminutive size, for she was a little wisp of a woman, Sr. M. Xaverius had no problems with discipline in the school of nursing, not because she was a stern, authority figure, but because she was a warm, approachable human being. Her practice of signing all memos to the students with her initials, SMX, earned her the nickname, "Smix," the name still used by St. Clare's graduates in referring to their former director.

Sr. M. Xaverius was loved by all nurses. No matter what her nurses did—within reason—she judged everyone by "ocular proof." If "Smix" didn't see the indiscretion, it didn't happen. There was the instance when a passerby was hit by a cigarette butt thrown from the nurses' residence. Smoking in the residence was strictly forbidden, which made it all the more tempting, and being young and daring, the students took their chances. One day, four nurses were smoking in a room on the third floor of the old residence on St. Clare Avenue, creating an atmosphere so thick it could be cut with a knife. Suddenly, there was a knock on the door. Quickly, the four culprits tossed the remains of their cigarettes through the open window. Sr. M. Xaverius entered, stopped and sniffed. She looked at the four students who were, by that time, seated at the table in front of open textbooks. Sister asked, "Do I smell smoke?" The four dutifully lifted their heads and sniffed in turn. "No, Sister." Just then the doorbell rang. Sr. M. Xaverius turned and went to answer the door to find a very indignant lady with a cigarette butt in her hand. The lady complained that it had been thrown from a window in the nurses' residence and had hit her on the head as she was passing the residence. Sister listened attentively to the lady's story, thought for a moment or two and then told her that she had no "ocular proof" that the cigarette butt had been thrown by one of her nurses—it could have been one of the workmen on the roof! Therefore, there was simply nothing she could do about it. The lady opened her mouth to point out that there were no workmen on the roof, but after one look at Sister's expression, she said nothing and departed in offended silence. The four nurses were called to Sr. M. Xaverius' office where she told them the lady's story. They stood silently, wondering what form of punishment was to be inflicted. Possibly no more "leave" for a month? After leaving them in suspense for a minute or so, Sister inquired, "Well, have you nothing better to do than stand there looking into space?" And the four delinquents beat a hasty retreat. No wonder the students loved their diminutive director!

At St. Clare's school of nursing, mornings began early with the clang of an electric bell at 6:00 AM. To the majority this meant, "jump" in order to be on time for the 6:40 roll call. The fact that the director was so tiny was a distinct advantage for those students who liked to steal a few extra minutes of sleep. Because Sr. M. Xaverius could not see over the heads of those who were in the front of the room, latecomers could always arrange with a friend to answer, "Present," leaving "Smix" blissfully unaware that some of her students were slumbering peacefully in their beds.

It should be remembered that in those days most young women who decided to enter the nursing profession enrolled in a nursing school almost immediately after graduating from high school. Thus, it might be expected that St. Clare's school of nursing was no stranger to more than a few youthful escapades. St. Jude's Hall (the fourth floor of the hospital) was the largest floor for medical and surgical nursing. The nurses assigned to night duty, which began at 7:00 PM, were served a meal at 10:00 PM then nothing more until breakfast. The student nurses were young enough to be always hungry, but they were never allowed to accept food from a patient. Although there was a kitchenette on each floor, all food supplies were kept in the basement kitchen and sent to the floor by means of a food lift when it was time to serve the patients.

One night, the nurses on duty were suffering more than usual from the pangs of hunger. With no food available in the kitchenette, they decided to raid the kitchen. The problem was how to get into the basement kitchen, where the door was locked every evening. Fortunately, one of the nurses on duty was a tiny little woman who weighed about ninety pounds. It was decided that if she would agree to go down on the lift, she could invade the kitchen pantry and come up with sufficient goodies to satisfy the needs of her starving companions. After some persuasion, and possibly a little blackmail, she agreed. She was stuffed in the lift and down she went into the depths of the hospital. She was told that when she had collected enough food to feed the nurses on the fourth floor, plus a couple of nurses from the case room (which was idle at the time), she was to knock on the lift. After a lengthy forage in the pantries of the dietary department, the little nurse knocked on the door of the food lift and her waiting companions pushed the button that would bring her up. Unfortunately, during the ascent, Sr. M. Aidan

Howell, the night supervisor at the time, decided to visit the kitchenette where she found three rather guilty-looking young nurses. Sr. M. Aidan was about to inquire why the nurses were not out on the floor with the patients when she heard a loud knocking and cries of, "Let me out! Let me out!" Quite alarmed, Sr. M. Aidan turned to investigate the source of the frantic cries for help that seemed to be coming from the food lift. She strode across the room, opened the door of the lift, and out popped the tiniest nurse in the hospital with enough food to feed the entire staff and most of the patients as well. "Well, well, well," said Sr. M. Aidan, and without another word, off she went to complete her rounds. Although the three young nurses waited in fear and trembling to be called to face Sr. M. Xaverius, the director of the school of nursing, as the days passed and nothing happened, they decided that Sr. M. Aidan had not reported the incident.[7]

On April 25, 1944, the St. Clare's Mercy Hospital School of Nursing Alumnae Association was formed with Lillian Coleman, a member of the first graduating class, as its president. In 1954, with the help of the alumnae association, sufficient funds were raised to send two students, Mary Collins and Hope Moakler, to attend the Twenty-Seventh Biennial Convention of the Canadian Nurses Association held that year at Banff, Alberta. This was the first of many activities sponsored by the alumnae association for the benefit of student nurses.

When affiliations with other health care institutions began in 1946, they were carried out toward the end of the second year and the beginning of the third year. Nurses rotated in small groups of three or four to three hospitals in the city. Students spent a month in the Hospital for Mental and

7. Bernadette (Mason) Weinhebcr (graduate, St. Clare's school of nursing, 1954), interview by the author, August 4, 2009. As a matter of fact, Sr. M. Aidan, who had a well-developed sense of humour, told Sr. M. Xaverius the whole story, much to the amusement of the latter.

Nervous Diseases, a month in the Sanatorium that cared for persons suffering from tuberculosis, and a month in the Fever Hospital for communicable diseases.[8] In 1959, nursing students from the General Hospital School of Nursing began a three-month affiliation in obstetrics at St. Clare's. During this experience, St. Clare's faculty and staff willingly accepted responsibility for the teaching and clinical practice of the General Hospital students.

Over the course of the years, other affiliations were initiated, for example, with the Victorian Order of Nurses, St. Patrick's Mercy Home, where students obtained experience in geriatric medicine, and in pediatrics at the Dr. Charles A. Janeway Child Health Centre. Affiliations for tuberculosis and communicable diseases discontinued in 1965, when nurse interns began an affiliation program in cottage hospitals at Old Perlican, Carbonear, St. Lawrence, Buchans, Placentia, Botwood, and Stephenville. The purpose of this experience was to help enrich the students' understanding of the available health care facilities and also to provide an awareness of the health needs in outlying districts. Negotiations were also under way at this time with the Department of Health to help facilitate student learning experience in the field of public health nursing. Arrangements were made also for a two-week affiliation at the General Hospital in orthopedic and neuro-surgical nursing. By 1989, St. Clare's students were affiliating in twelve different health care institutions.

Meanwhile, in 1957, Sr. M. Calasanctius Power was appointed director of nursing education. With the appointment of a director, nursing education at St. Clare's became more organized and the need for additional classroom space and residence facilities became critical. Plans for new residence were in the works, as the subject had been brought up the previous year. At a meeting of the St. Clare's board of governors on July 20,

---

8. Eventually, the psychiatric affiliation was increased to two months.

1956, it was brought to the attention of the board that assistance to build a new nurses' residence could be obtained from the federal government on condition that the provincial government and the hospital would match the grant: five hundred dollars for every bed and one hundred dollars for every three hundred square feet of classroom, office, and auditorium space. It was proposed by Right Reverend Monsignor Harold Summers that the administrator of the hospital make a tentative approach to the provincial government through the minister of health, Dr. James McGrath, for information in reference to this grant.[9] It was the first time in its history that St. Clare's Mercy Hospital applied for a government grant to help finance a new student residence. At the next meeting of the board of governors, Sr. M. Fabian reported that Dr. McGrath had been interviewed but could give no definite information regarding the provincial portion of the grant until the executive council had met.[10] And there the matter rested. The minutes record no further word from the provincial government with reference to its share of the grant. The problem of providing accommodation for student nurses needed an immediate solution, but unless the provincial government provided its share of the grant, it was impossible to proceed with the plan for a new student residence.

Having exhausted all earthly avenues, the sisters sought heavenly assistance! A novena in honour of Our Lady of Lourdes was begun in St. Clare's Convent, and for nine days the sisters stormed heaven.[11] The novena concluded on February 11, the day on which the Church celebrates the Feast of Our Lady of Lourdes. That morning, Sr. M. Fabian Hennebury, the hospital administrator, received a phone call from Dr. James McGrath,

---

9. Minutes, Board of Governors of St. Clare's Mercy Hospital (hereafter cited as BOGSC), July 20, 1956, ASMSJ.

10. Minutes, BOGSC, October 2, 1956, ASMSJ.

11. A novena consists of a prayer that is offered to God for nine consecutive days. The prayer is usually offered in honour of the Virgin Mary or some saint.

the minister of health, informing her that the grant was available to St. Clare's.[12] However, under the terms of the grant, the hospital had to find the money to cover its share of the cost. The only solution was to take out a bank loan. In those days, Roman Catholic women religious were obliged by Canon Law to have permission of the Vatican before taking out a sizeable loan. Therefore, it was decided by the board that the administrator, Sr. M. Fabian, would write to Rome for this permission. The following is a copy of the letter sent to the Holy Father:

The Superintendent of St. Clare's Mercy Hospital in St. John's, Newfoundland . . . implores permission to obtain a bank loan of $290,000.00 in order to erect a new nurses' home at St. Clare's Mercy Hospital.

Present Nurses' Home:

St. Clare's Mercy Hospital was built in 1939 and extended in 1948. Two private dwellings behind the hospital were acquired and joined together to serve as the first Nurses' Residence. In 1946 an extension was constructed and joined to the other two houses. Finally in 1954 another private home . . . was acquired, but not joined to the existing structure.

Overcrowding is serious with ninety nurses in residence. Student nurses sleep in dormitories with beds so close together that there is no room for either screens or partitions. The fire hazard is very great because

(a) of overcrowding;

(b) the residence is made of wood;

(c) the lack of adequate fire escapes;

(d) the complicated arrangement of rooms and stairs because of the fact that the structure began with two private dwelling houses. [13]

---

12. Hennebury, "St. Clare's," ASMSJ, 37.
13. Minutes, BOGSC, February 22, 1957, ASMSJ.

In the remainder of this letter, Sr. M. Fabian described the proposed construction of a new residence, the method of financing, and the financial arrangements.[14] Then, on February 25, three days later, the provincial government confirmed in writing that its share of the grant would be available to build a residence for student nurses. Construction began early in the spring, and the residence, known as Our Lady of Lourdes Hall, was officially blessed and opened on September 24, 1958.

Prior to the opening of the new residence, the average number of students entering the school of nursing was thirty-five; however, with the opening of the new school, the number increased to fifty-two. The educational program at this time was revised to meet the changing standards of nursing education, the first priority being organization of the school faculty. An executive committee was formed comprising three standing committees: curriculum committee, health committee, and library and finance committee.

The basic diploma course still covered a period of three years and included physical and biological science, social sciences, medical sciences, nursing and allied arts. The curriculum of the school combined formal teaching with an organized clinical program as the students learned to correlate theory and practice. One interesting feature of the program was the emphasis on nutrition. Each student nurse was required to spend six weeks in the dietary department under the supervision of Sr. M. Andrea Sutton. The importance of proper diet and nutrition was considered an essential component in the recovery of patients suffering from various illnesses. Needless to say, this part of the training was very popular with the students who did not hesitate to avail of the opportunity to sample various delicacies not available in the student cafeteria.[15]

Student involvment at St. Clare's Mercy Hospital School

14. Ibid.

15. The author is indebted to Mrs. Harriet (Boland) Doyle for this information.

of Nursing was always encouraged. The more literary-minded among the students decided that the school of nursing should publish a yearbook. Members of the first editorial staff were elected: Margaret Lynch, Margaret Scott,[16] and Jenny McDonald. These three set to work, and the first issue of the yearbook was published in 1953—a simple little book with a rather imposing title, "Claretian." It was well-received, and its publication was the responsibility of each graduating class during the years that followed.

As enrollment increased, Sr. M. Xaverius decided that it was time the students took a more active part in the running of the school. The Student Government Association was inaugurated in 1958 and a constitution and bylaws drawn up. An executive committee and three sub-committees were formed.

Sr. M. Xaverius suggested to the student government that they issue a musical challenge to the students, an idea that was embraced with enthusiasm. Sr. M. Edward Hodge and Sr. M. Celine Veitch, two very competent musicians, were asked to start singing classes with the students. And so, St. Clare's Mercy Hospital Glee Club was formed. The choir performed at all the school's graduations for many years. In addition, the choir presented spring concerts, and in 1968, a special group from the choir won the Inter-School Championship Award for the best dramatic performance during Newfoundland Students' Day.

Another project initiated by the student government was delegated to the junior students, who, at the approach of Christmas, collected enough food and clothing to fill twelve hampers for needy families. This practice multiplied and extended to the hospital departments over the years, and many dozens of hampers were made ready each Christmas through the generosity of the employees and volunteer workers.

In 1959, the third-year students had the privilege of a free

---

16. Margaret Scott, having completed the requirements as a registered nurse, later qualified as a medical doctor.

air-trip to Greenwood, NS, sponsored by the RCAF. Two of the students who participated in this project, Leona Waddleton and Margaret Jackman, joined the air force after graduating in 1960. They became staff members at the Royal Canadian Air Force hospital at Queensway, Ottawa, and served there for several years. This recruitment initiative by the RCAF continued for several years. In 1964, a group of about thirty student nurses from the General Hospital, the Grace General Hospital, and St. Clare's Mercy Hospital schools of nursing were invited to spend a couple of days touring the Canadian Forces facilities in Nova Scotia. Ten representatives from St. Clare's participated. The eight students—Judith Adams, Cavell Bennett, Harriet Boland, Mary Coleman, Jeanette Crocker, Catherine Francis, Mary Gosse, and Mary Hearn—were accompanied by two registered nurses, Mary Philpott and Barbara Kelly. The visitors were treated royally—they lunched in the officers wardroom on HMCS *Stadacona*[17] and later that same day were entertained at dinner on the same boat. During the two days they spent in Nova Scotia, the students had the opportunity of visiting the Canadian Forces Hospital in Halifax and touring the RCAF Station in Greenwood.[18]

The 1960s brought a period of change. The opening of the new obstetrical wing of the hospital in January 1962 provided the students with the privilege of learning in a bright new facility which helped to enhance care for the mother and child.

In January 1961, the administration of the school agreed to participate in the Canadian Nurses' Association Improvement Program. This exercise presented an indication of the strengths and weaknesses in terms of the curriculum,

---

17. HMCS *Stadacona* was a commissioned patrol boat of the Royal Canadian Navy and was one of the many ships to serve in World War I and World War II.

18. The author is indebted to Mrs. Harriet (Boland) Doyle for this information.

administration, management, and organization of the school of nursing. Also in 1961, on completion of the three-year program, the students wrote the United States State Board Test Pool Examination, a requisite for registration in this province. This was arranged by the executive of the Association of Registered Nurses of Newfoundland and was continued until 1970, when a national Canadian examination was developed. This examination was written for the first time in August 1970. The pass mark, which reflects a standard score rather than a percentage, was 200. After 1973, it was changed to 350.

In 1963, in response to the need for updating the curriculum a "Two Year Plus One Program" was introduced and developed by the faculty. It was approved and accepted by the Association of Registered Nurses of Newfoundland. The students were to be provided with two years of theory and one year of nurse internship. During the 1960s, Canadian nursing schools were responding to a nationwide school improvement program. The program adopted at St. Clare's embraced the latest educational concepts used in programs across Canada.

At the same time, a ten-month course for nursing assistants was implemented. The course consisted of three months of classroom teaching and seven months of clinical practice and supervision. At the end of the course, the student received a diploma and pin and was recognized as a certified nursing assistant. This course was later replaced by a certified course for nursing assistants who had trained in special areas of mental health and tuberculosis nursing.

On November 10, 1965, a meeting was held at Memorial University to discuss the placement of university nursing students at St. Clare's for the purpose of obtaining clinical experience. An agreement was reached with Memorial University, and an inter-agency committee was established to control the placement of students for this experience. Memorial University established a medical school in 1967, and in 1968, St. Clare's became a teaching hospital in affiliation with the Memorial University of Newfoundland, and since that time, it has provided clinical teaching and experience to students, interns, and residents in the various medical disciplines.

In 1970, a joint committee with representation from the three diploma schools of nursing in St. John's was established to review curriculum and to make recommendations to the schools regarding courses and clinical experience.[19] The purpose of these joint committees was to assist faculty members to plan programs in all schools of nursing that would lead to better utilization of existing facilities. The joint planning committee focused its attention on maternity, pediatric, and psychiatric nursing.

One of the significant events of the decade of the 1970s was the retirement of the director of the school, Sr. M. Xaverius (Catherine) Kenny in 1974. A year earlier, Sr. M. Xaverius had reverted to her baptismal name, Catherine. The change was not quite as confusing as it might seem, for students and alumnae continued to refer to her as "Smix."

However, Sr. Catherine Kenny had not finished with St. Clare's. After her retirement from St. Clare's Mercy Hospital School of Nursing she was appointed secretary-general of the Sisters of Mercy. After her term of office was completed, she returned to St. Clare's in 1981 to establish the St. Clare's Mercy Hospital School of Nursing Archives. She began her valuable work as she briefed herself with an old saying: "An institution must have a memory if it is to be conscious of itself." Her work entailed the collection as well as the preservation of the school's scattered records with its forty-three years of historical events. A large album contains an overall pictorial view of the happenings from the hospital's beginnings in 1922 to the 1980s. Graduates of St. Clare's Mercy Hospital School of Nursing who visit the

---

19. The General Hospital, St. Clare's Mercy Hospital, and the Grace General Hospital.

archives view with enthusiasm the display and other memorabilia that recall the past and evoke pardonable pride in their rich heritage. These visits often result in the telling and re-telling of stories in which the memory of Sr. Catherine Kenny, "Smix," is recalled with love and respect.

In 1974, when it was announced to the students that Sr. Catherine Kenny was due to retire as director of the school of nursing, the news was received with real regret. It was hard to imagine St. Clare's school of nursing without "Smix" as director. However, the concerns of students were put to rest when news spread around the hospital that Mrs. Kathrine Daley had been appointed as the new director of St. Clare's Mercy Hospital School of Nursing. The appointment of Katherine (Kay) Daley to replace Sr. Catherine Kenny as director proved to be a blessing for St. Clare's and for nursing education in general.

Prior to her appointment as director of St. Clare's Mercy Hospital School of Nursing, Kay Daley had been the first director of the school of nursing at Western Memorial Hospital in Corner Brook, established in 1968. A graduate of St. Joseph's Hospital School of Nursing in Nova Scotia, Kay Daley also had obtained a diploma in nursing education from Dalhousie University and a bachelor of arts, bachelor of education, and masters of education from Memorial University of Newfoundland. Furthermore, she was an experienced, wise, and forward-looking woman. In light of the changes in nursing education that were taking place on an almost monthly basis, she was the right person in the right place.

In 1977, the Canadian Nurses Association Testing Services released the blueprint for a new comprehensive examination that was to take effect in 1980. Up to this time, registration examinations for nurses in Canada had been divided into areas of specialization and had been used to evaluate the minimum abilities of candidates seeking entry to the profession; that is, students wrote five registration exam-inations—medical, surgical, obstetrics, pediatrics, and psychi-atric nursing. The concept underlying this type of examina-tion had been somewhat discredited in favour of a compre-hensive, fully integrated single examination approach. In August 1980, the third-year students at St. Clare's school of nursing joined all other nursing students in Canada in the ini-tial writing of this examination. Forty of forty-one students writing the examination were successful.

During the period of the 1980s, there were greater demands for registered nurses. Applications for entrance to the program increased from approximately two hundred appli-cants a year in the 1970s to almost four hundred by the end of the decade. One noticeable change was the increased number of mature students applying for admission to the school. The largest class, consisting of ninety-four students, was accepted in 1982. With increased enrolments, the demand for accommo-dation became a major concern of the school. During 1980, a joint proposal from the Grace General Hospital School of Nursing and St. Clare's Mercy Hospital School of Nursing was made to the Department of Health regarding the feasibility of using St. Bride's College, Littledale, for first-year students from both schools. The proposal was approved by the govern-ment,[20] and in September of 1980, thirty students from each school of nursing registered at Creedon Residence, Littledale.

Beginning in the 1980s and continuing throughout the decade, the profile of students entering the school changed. Fewer high school students and more mature students became interested in nursing. By the late 1980s, almost one half of the student population at St. Clare's was over twenty-one years of age. Also, throughout this decade, students and faculty from St. Clare's school of nursing distinguished themselves in many areas. For instance, in 1983, two faculty members, Joan Marie

---

20. Minutes, BOGSC, May 27, 1980, ASMSJ.

Aylward[21] and Deborah Duff, wrote and published *A Metric Guide for Health Professionals on Dosages and Solutions.* This text was a first for Canada and is presently in its second edition.

Another interesting event took place in 1984 when Laura Elizabeth Smith graduated from St. Clare's. Laura was the fifth daughter of Theresa (Downey) Smith to study nursing at St. Clare's. During the graduation ceremony, Mrs. Smith, who was herself a graduate of St. Clare's (class of 1951), presented her youngest daughter with her diploma.

Even though the first-year students had been moved to Littledale in 1980, within a few years it became obvious that the 1958 building that housed the school of nursing was no longer adequate to meet the needs of the nursing students at St. Clare's. Our Lady of Lourdes Hall had been built to accommodate one hundred students and a faculty of three. In 1990, the school had an enrollment of almost two hundred and fifty students and a faculty and support staff of twenty to twenty-five full- and part-time teachers. The board of governors of St. Clare's and Katherine Daley, the director of the school of nursing, realized that either another, larger site or a new building would have to be provided for the school of nursing. They did not have far to look for the larger site. Because the former St. Bride's College on Littledale complex had been designed and built to function as a residential college, it was provided with facilities which were ideal for post-secondary educational programs. In addition to the required residence facilities, the administrative, educational, and recreational features of the complex met all the requirements of the school of nursing. Furthermore, the complex boasted spacious classrooms, conference areas, a state-of-the-art audiovisual theatre, and a

---

21. Subsequently, Joan Marie Aylward became president of the Newfoundland and Labrador Nurses Union (NLNU). Later still, she ran for political office and filled two important positions in cabinet, first as minister of health and then minister of finance.

library. Situated in the beautiful Waterford Valley, the quiet, park-like setting made the complex an ideal environment for the school of nursing. Early in 1990, the government approved the relocation of St. Clare's school of nursing to the Littledale campus.[22] And so, in August 1990, the St. Clare's Mercy Hospital School of Nursing moved to the building formerly occupied by St. Bride's College. The formal opening took place on November 5, 1990.

However, time never stands still. The 1990s was, in the planning manuals of the Newfoundland government, a time for consolidation. As early as December 1991, the nursing education advisory committee circulated a report to the executive officers of the hospitals recommending that a centralized school of nursing be formed under one board and away from hospitals.[23] This suggestion was taken seriously by the government, and in 1994, the budget speech mentioned consolidation of the schools of nursing.[24] The directors of the schools of nursing were quick to act. In September 1994, the minutes of the meeting of the board of governors of St. Clare's contain the following:

> Dr. Conroy [Acting Executive Director of St. Clare's] reported that the committee representing the three diploma Schools of Nursing presented four options to the Minister of Health [Lloyd Matthews]. The fourth option: to consolidate the Schools of Nursing using a phased-in approach . . . is the option that the committee recommends in that it would achieve the overall goal of linking the consolidation with the broader Board restructuring for St. John's [25] and the implementation of a collaborative curriculum. This is a unique

22. Minutes, BOGSC, April 26, 1990, ASMSJ.
23. Minutes, BOGSC, December 5, 1991, ASMSJ.
24. Minutes, BOGSC, March 24, 1994, ASMSJ.
25. By this time, the government had implemented a plan to unite all the St. John's hospitals under one umbrella—the Health Care Corporation of St. John's. This development is discussed at length in chapter 11.

approach, and the first of its kind in Canada. A committee made of the representatives from the province's five Schools of Nursing has coordinated the development of a new curriculum for a baccalaureate program in nursing.[26]

By 1995, the government, the hospitals, and the schools of nursing had come to a final agreement. On October 27, 1995, Sr. Phyllis Corbett, the administrator of St. Clare's Mercy Hospital, reported to the board that the report on the consolidation of diploma schools of nursing had been submitted to the minister of health with the recommendation that the consolidation be achieved by using a phased-in approach to be completed by September 1998.[27] Subsequently, this recommendation was accepted by the government, and in September 1996, the three diploma nursing schools in St. John's were merged under one umbrella, the Centre for Nursing Studies. Katherine Daley, the former director of St. Clare's Mercy Hospital School of Nursing was appointed director of the new centre. The opening of the Centre for Nursing Studies and the establishment of the bachelor of nursing (collaborative) program with the province's other two schools of nursing marked an important milestone in the history of nursing education in the province. Furthermore, a department of continuing nursing studies was established at the Centre for Nursing Studies to respond to the need for postgraduate education.[28]

On June 25, 1998, the final graduation ceremony of St. Clare's Mercy Hospital School of Nursing took place at the St. John's Arts and Culture Centre. The following day, June 26, a

26. Minutes, BOGSC, September 24, 1994, ASMSJ.

27. Minutes, BOGSC, October 27, 1995, ASMSJ.

28. After her retirement from the Centre for Nursing Studies, Katherine Daley established the Newfoundland and Labrador Health and Community Services Archive and Museum. This organization is dedicated to discovering, collecting, and preserving the history of health care in the province of Newfoundland and Labrador.

special ceremony was held to mark the formal closing of the school. On this occasion, Sr. Charlotte Fitzpatrick, the congregational leader of the Sisters of Mercy, addressed the gathering as follows:

> On February 19, 1941 . . . five women became the first graduates of the school, a vanguard of a long line of women and men reaching down through six decades of time . . . The values learned and lived at the school, the high standards of scholarship and clinical expertise, the wise mentoring, the enthusiasm and expertise of dedicated teachers created and enabled a learning environment that made St. Clare's School of Nursing a school of life . . . The story of St. Clare's will continue to live in the legacy it has passed on—in the lives of the 2,296 graduates of St. Clare's who have been part of the healing ministry in Newfoundland and across the world . . . Today as we celebrate and give thanks for the life and ministry of the St. Clare's School of Nursing, we recognize that we are on the threshold of a new moment where the future is wide open, where untold possibilities exist. We are grateful for the past with all its achievements and moments of glory, and we bring all of that with us, enriched by it and better prepared to move into the future.[29]

The closing of St. Clare's Mercy Hospital School of Nursing did not pass unnoticed by the Health Care Corporation of St. John's. In a message to the graduates, Sr. Elizabeth Davis, chief executive officer of the Health Care Corporation wrote:

> These are days to grieve and to celebrate—to grieve the closing of your School of Nursing and to celebrate the legacy

---

29. Sr. Charlotte Fitzpatrick, Address given at the closing ceremony of St. Clare's Mercy Hospital School of Nursing, St. John's, June 26, 1998, ASMSJ.

your School has left . . . "Misericordia Super Omnia—Mercy Above All" is the theme of your School imprinted on your pins and rings and, most especially, on your spirit of nursing. This theme best describes the legacy which your School has left this province, the nursing profession, the places you have been, and you, yourself.

In this province, the St. Clare's School of Nursing has left its mark on every one of our hospitals, nursing homes and community-based agencies. It has influenced the Association of Registered Nurses of Newfoundland, the Newfoundland and Labrador Nurses' Union and many nurses' special interest groups. Its graduates have made a difference in the Department of Health and Community Services, the Department of Human Resources and Employment, and other government departments as well as in municipal governments.

The nursing profession has been strengthened because St. Clare's School of Nursing existed. Through nursing education and nursing research as well as through nursing service, St. Clare's graduates have helped shape a nursing profession in this province that has kept the patient or resident or client always at the centre, a nursing profession which is progressive, caring and competent.

And the St. Clare's School of Nursing has made a difference wherever you, its graduates, have been present. In cottage hospitals and tertiary centres, in nursing homes and educational settings, in nursing clinics and occupational health centres, in clients' homes, in senior management teams and government departments, on boards of trustees and in advocacy groups, you have brought gifts of wisdom, competence and compassion.

Now you say farewell to the School which has nurtured these gifts in you. May its legacy live through you and in the persons whose lives you touch. May its legacy strengthen the foundation of the Centre for Nursing Studies which now carries on its mission. May the spirit of St. Clare's School of Nursing continue in all those nurses whose work is marked by "Mercy Above All—Misericordia Super Omnia."[30]

---

30. Elizabeth M. Davis, RSM, chief executive officer, Health Care Corporation of St. John's, Address given at the closing ceremony of St. Clare's Mercy Hospital School of Nursing, St. John's, June 26, 1998, ASMSJ.

Catherine McAuley, foundress of the Sisters of Mercy

Sketch by Willie Brandts showing Sisters of Mercy caring for victims of the cholera epidemic of 1856 (courtesy of CBC, St. John's)

Archbishop E. P. Roche, archbishop of St. John's, 1915–1950

St. Clare's Mercy Hospital was opened at the request of and under the guidance of Archbishop Roche, who remained deeply involved in the growth of the hospital until his death in 1950.

Most Reverend Michael F. Howley, bishop of St. John's, 1895–1904; archbishop of St. John's, 1904–1914

Archbishop Howley intended to open a Catholic hospital under the care of the Sisters of Mercy but died before he could bring his plan to fruition.

St. Clare's Mercy Hospital, 1922

Sr. M. Bernard Gladney, RN, first administrator of St. Clare's Mercy Hospital, 1922

Sr. M. Bridget O'Connor, superior general of the Sisters of Mercy when St. Clare's Mercy Hospital opened, 1922

Alice Casey (Higgins), RN, first registered nurse to work at St. Clare's Mercy Hospital with Sr. M. Bernard Gladney, 1922–1923

Dr. John Murphy, first chief of staff of St. Clare's Mercy Hospital

Sr. M. Aloysius Rawlins, RN,
administrator, St. Clare's Mercy
Hospital, 1923–1931, 1937–1951

St. Clare's Mercy Hospital, 1939 building, with the 1950 chapel
building on the left

First Board of Directors of St. Clare's Mercy Hospital, 1939
Upper (l–r): Marcella O'Connor, Sr. M. Stanislaus Parsons
Lower (l–r): Sr. M. Bridget O'Connor, Archbishop E. P. Roche, Sr.M.
Aloysius Rawlins

Dr. Garret M. Brownrigg, CBE, president of the medical advisory
committee, 1958; chief of medical staff, 1958–1977; chief of surgery, 1958–1977

First graduation class, St. Clare's Mercy Hospital School of Nursing, 1941, (l–r): Ethel Goff, Eileen O'Brien, Anne Hogan, May O'Rielly, Lillian Coleman

Brenda Simms and Angela Maher, flower girls at St. Clare's Mercy Hospital School of Nursing graduation, 1958

First medical advisory committee, 1956
Upper (l–r): Dr. J. B. Murphy, Dr. G. M. Brownrigg, Dr. R. J. Simms
Lower (l–r): Dr. T. G. Anderson, Dr. F. L. O'Dea

Board of Governors of St. Clare's Mercy Hospital, 1958, (clockwise from lower left): Sr. M. Loretta McIsaac, Monsignor Harold Summers, Robert Furlong, Archbishop P. J. Skinner, Monsignor Edward Maher, Sr. M. Fabian Hennebury, Sr. M. Assumpta Veitch

Medical advisory committee, 1960
Standing (l–r): Dr. G. Battcock, Dr. K. Linegar, Dr. A. Morris, Dr. B.
Higgins, Dr. J. Seviour
Seated (l–r): Dr. J. Williams, Dr. R. Simms, Dr. G. Brownrigg

Chapel, St. Clare's Mercy Hospital

St. Clare's Mercy Hospital School of Nursing, 1958

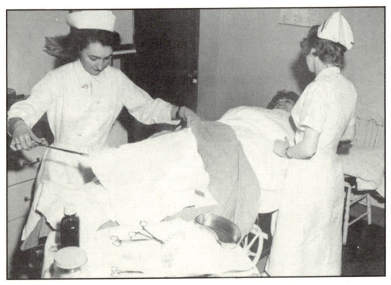

Nursing experience in the emergency room

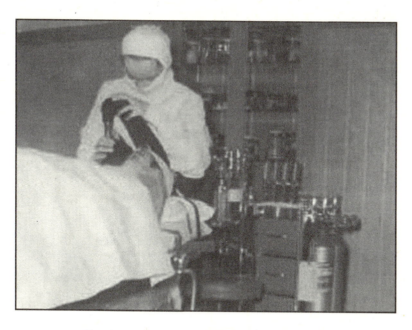

Nursing experience in the operating rooms

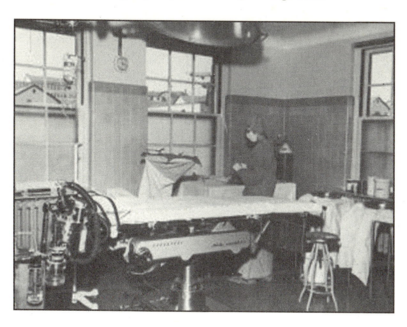

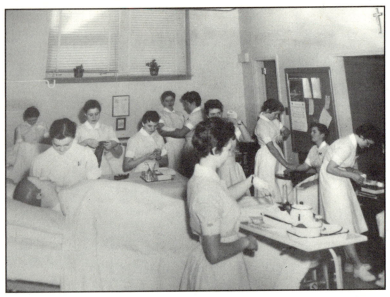

Student practice, St. Clare's Mercy Hospital School of Nursing, c. 1960

St. Clare's Mercy Hospital, 1962 extension on St. Clare Avenue

Sr. M. Carmelita Hartman, who came to St. Clare's in 1923 during the illness of Sr. M. Bernard Gladney

Sr. M. Stanislaus Parsons, RN, first director of St. Clare's Mercy Hospital School of Nursing, 1939–1944

Sr. M. Magdalen Baker, RN, supervisor of the radiology department; first registered X-ray technologist in Newfoundland; founding member of the Society of Radiological Technologists

Marcella O'Connor, RN, director of nursing services, St. Clare's Mercy Hospital, 1925

Sr. M. Loretta McIsaac, RN, anaesthetist and supervisor of the operating room, 1929–1950

Sr. M. Xaverius Kenny, RN, director of St. Clare's Mercy Hospital School of Nursing, 1943–1974

Sr. M. Fabian Hennebury, RN, administrator of St. Clare's Mercy Hospital, 1955–1981

Sr. M. Brenda Lacey, RN, medical records, St. Clare's Mercy Hospital, 1957–1989

Sr. M. Rosarii O'Brien, RN, nursing supervisor, c. 1963

Ann Summers, RN, Miss St. Clare's, 1963

Sr. M. Andrea Sutton, dietary department

Sr. Marian Grace Manning, RN, prepares patient for the operating room

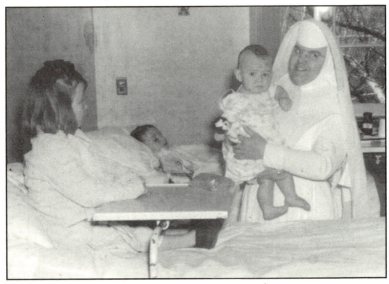

Sr. M. Aidan Howell, RN, with sick children in pediatrics

St. Clare's Mercy Hospital, 1972 extension

St. Clare's Mercy Hospital, 1972, with Church of St. Michael and All Angels (top right)

Opening of palliative care unit, St. Clare's Mercy Hospital, October 1, 1979, (l–r): Sr. M. Fabian Hennebury; Archbishop Alphonsus L. Penney; Laurie Anne O'Brien; Aidan Maloney; Monsignor David P. Morrissey; Reverend James Glavine, CSsR

Opening of the CT (computed tomography) scanner, St. Clare's
Mercy Hospital, June 6, 1991

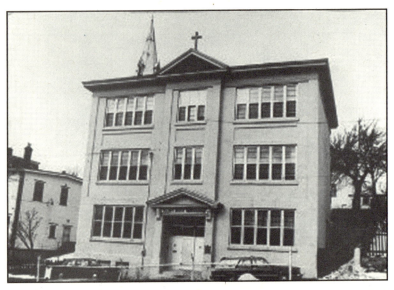

Talbot House, Deanery Avenue, 1978–1999

Sr. Patricia Marie Decker and members of the dietary department, c. 1970

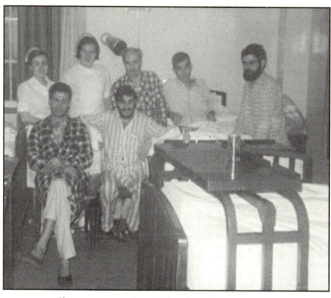

Portuguese sailors recovering from lead poisoning at St. Clare's Mercy Hospital with nurses (l–r) Shirley Kenny (nurse intern) and Helen Lawlor, RN

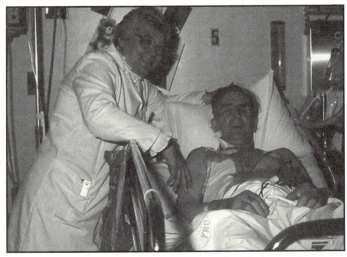

Sr. Irene Kennedy, pastoral care, with patient in intensive care unit

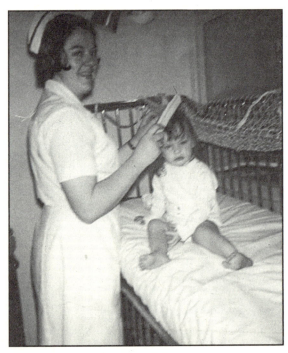

"My hair is a mess!" Pediatric beauty parlour, Kay Boggan, RN, with patient

Katherine Daley, RN, director, St. Clare's Mercy Hospital School of Nursing, 1974–1995

Lucy (Power) Dobbin, RN, executive director, St. Clare's Mercy Hospital, 1982–1986

Theresa Downey Smith and her five daughters, all graduates of St. Clare's Mercy Hospital School of Nursing, (clockwise from top left): Sheila, Carolyn, Theresa, Christina, Paula, Laura, 1984

Sr. M. Jude O'Grady, RN, director of pastoral care, 1983–1986

Sr. Patricia Maher presenting the Sisters of Mercy 150th anniversary scholarship to Eva Nash, RN

Deborah Duff, RN, and Joan Marie Aylward, RN, with publication *A Metric Guide for Health Professionals on Dosages and Solutions*, 1983

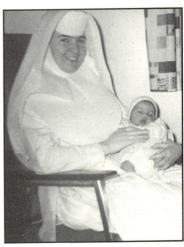

Sr. Rosaline Hynes with newborn baby

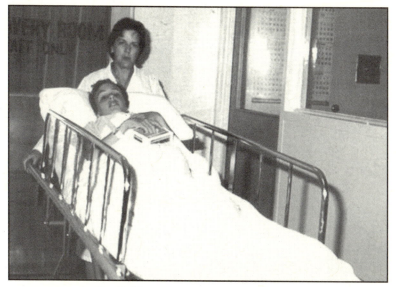

Sr. Callista Ryan, RNA, with patient

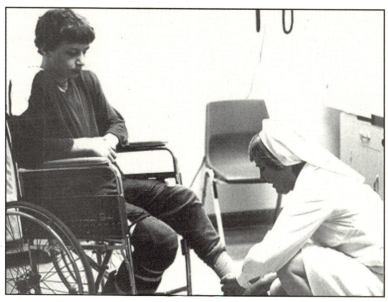

Sr. Jane McGrath, RN, in emergency department

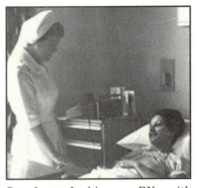

Sr. Jean Jenkinson, RN, with patient

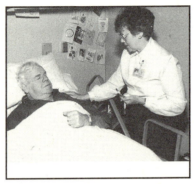

Sr. Ida Pomroy offering a patient Communion

Margaret Armstrong Kearney, first baby girl born at St. Clare's Mercy Hospital, February 6, 1925

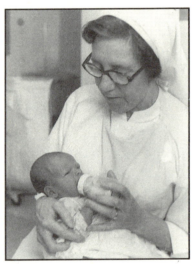

Sr. M. Antonia Carroll, RN, caring for infant in the nursery

Senior management meeting, 1993, (clockwise from lower left): Dr. Linda Hensman; Mr. Stephen Dodge; Sr. Phyllis Corbett, RN; Sr. Elizabeth Davis; Mrs. Barbara Legge-Pike; Mr. John McGrath; Dr. Sean Conroy

The last two Sisters of Mercy to graduate from St. Clare's Mercy Hospital School of Nursing, (l–r): Sr. Loretta Walsh, RN, 1983, and Sr. Eileen Penney, RN, 1993

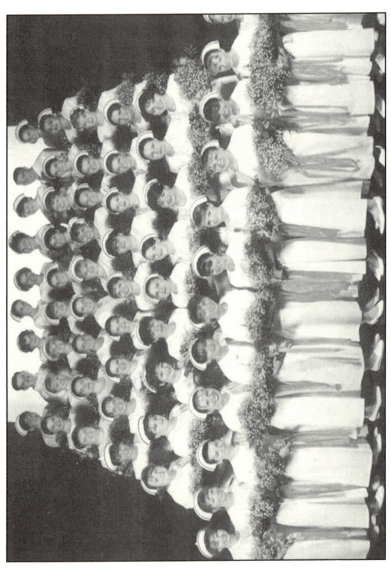

St. Clare's Mercy Hospital School of Nursing, last graduation class, 1998

First and last babies born at St. Clare's Mercy Hospital—Dr. Arthur Morris, 1924, and Daniel O'Neill, 1992 (shown with his mother, Michelle)

Sr. Madonna O'Neill, pastoral care, with patient

Opening of LeMarchant House, 1994, (l–r): Ann Curtis (manager), Aidan Maloney (board chairman), Sr. Charlotte Fitzpatrick

Sr. Marion Collins, superior general of the Sisters of Mercy in 1995 when St. Clare's Mercy Hospital was sold to the Newfoundland government

Sr. M. Calasanctius Power, RN, director of nursing education, St. Clare's Mercy Hospital School of Nursing, 1957–1962

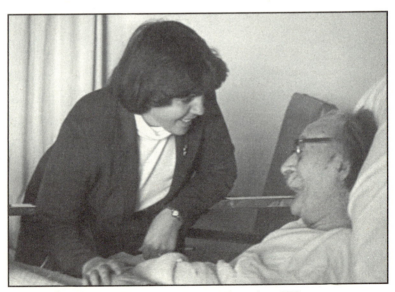

Sr. Diane Smyth, social work, 1979

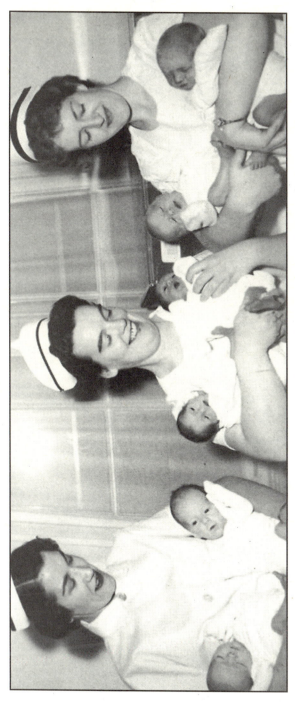

Three sets of twins held by nurses (l–r) Regina Horan, Anne McDonald, and Alice Molloy

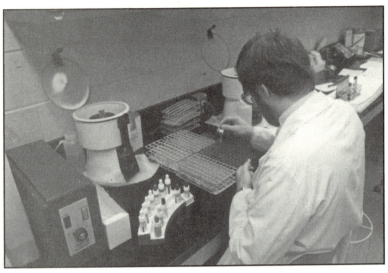

Laboratory, St. Clare's Mercy Hospital, c. 1995

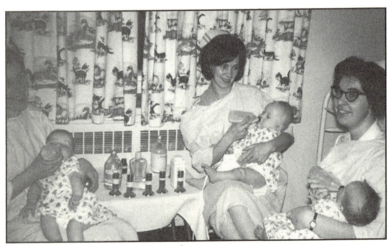

Dinnertime in pediatrics with nurses (l–r) Theresa Goodland, Judy Smith, and Harriet Boland

St. Clare's Mercy Hospital becomes part of the Health Care Corporation of St. John's, (l–r): Honourable Lloyd Matthews, minister of health, and Mr. Aidan Maloney, chairman of the Board of Governors of St. Clare's Mercy Hospital, March 25, 1995

The last meeting of the Board of Governors of St. Clare's Mercy Hospital, March 30, 1995

Dr. David Peddle, chief of staff, 1995

Aidan Maloney, chairman, Board of Governors of St. Clare's Mercy Hospital, 1989–1995

Judy Chubbs, RN (sitting), director of nursing services, with Sr. Phyllis Corbett, RN (standing), director of nursing, St. Clare's Mercy Hospital, 1995

Sr. Madonna Gatherall, director of mission effectiveness, St. Clare's Mercy Hospital and St. Patrick's Mercy Home, 1990–present

Sr. Elizabeth Davis, executive director, St. Clare's Mercy Hospital, 1986–1994

Environmental services, St. Clare's Mercy Hospital, c. 2005

St. Clare's Mercy Hospital pastoral care team, 2009
Back (l–r): Sr. Betty Morrissey, Reverend Jean Smith, Marie Ryall, Reverend Florence Sanna
Front (l–r): Sr. Eileen Flynn, Sr. M. Carmelita Power, Sr. Madonna Gatherall, Sr. Elizabeth Marrie, Sr. Diane Smyth, Sr. Madonna O'Neill

Front lobby mural by Gerry and Esther Squires

The Mustard Seed

Front lobby mural by Gerry and Esther Squires

Front lobby mural by Gerry and Esther Squires

St. Clare, patron saint of St. Clare's Mercy Hospital

Coming of Age

It is for us to pray not for tasks equal to our powers, but for powers equal to our tasks.

—Helen Keller

When the new St. Clare's Mercy Hospital opened in 1939, a board of directors was set up with Archbishop E. P. Roche as chairman.[1] Other members of the board included the superior general of the Sisters of Mercy, Sr. M. Bridget O'Connor; the administrator of the hospital, Sr. M. Aloysius Rawlins; the director of nursing, Sr. M. Stanislaus Parsons; and Marcella O'Connor, RN. However, there are no records of this board having met more than once. To all intents and purposes, during the years 1940–1950, Archbishop Roche appeared to have jurisdiction over much of the financial operation of the hospital and was a regular visitor to the hospital. There was no functioning board of directors or organized medical staff.[2]

Although the medical staff was not organized, Dr. J. B. Murphy was considered chief of staff and his advice was sought on all medical matters. The accounting system simply recorded income and expenditures, which included the expenses of St. Clare's Convent with the exception of personal items for the sisters, such as clothing. These costs were covered by the Congregation of the Sisters of Mercy. The sisters' accounts were

---

1. When the new 1939 St. Clare's Mercy Hospital was opened, a board of directors was established. When, in 1956, the critical need for a functioning board of directors was recognized, this body was called the Board of Governors of St. Clare's Mercy Hospital.
2. Hennebury, "St. Clare's," ASMSJ, 34.

not kept separate until the advent of health insurance in 1958, when the sisters received salaries for the first time.

From 1923 to 1951, with the exception of a six-year period (1931-1937), Sr. M. Aloysius Rawlins served as administrator of St. Clare's. These were the years when the hospital operated without any government assistance but depended solely on fees for services, the support of the Congregation of the Sisters of Mercy, and donations from friends of St. Clare's. It was under the wise and capable management of Sr. M. Aloysius Rawlins that St. Clare's earned its reputation for excellence in health care and for compassionate ministry to the sick. Operating on the proverbial shoestring, Sr. M. Aloysius Rawlins guided the hospital through the years of quiet growth that prepared a strong foundation for the major expansion of the 1960s and 1970s.

Early in 1950, it was discovered that the seemingly indestructible administrator of St. Clare's, Sr. M. Aloysius Rawlins, was suffering from a terminal illness. Because she had enjoyed excellent health all her life, nobody could imagine St. Clare's without Sr. M. Aloysius' energetic presence. However, the superiors of the Mercy congregation were forced to face the seriousness of the situation. Sr. M. Carmelita Hartigan was sent away to Mercy Hospital in Baltimore to study hospital administration and, after Sr. M. Aloysius died in November 1951, Sr. M. Carmelita was appointed administrator. Sadly, Sr. M. Carmelita was not destined to fill the position for any length of time. Shortly after her appointment, it was discovered that she had an aggressive form of cancer. On October 15, 1954, Sr. M. Carmelita died, leaving the position of administrator vacant. In the interim, before the appointment of a new administrator, Sr. M. Loretta McIsaac agreed to act in that position. The archbishop of St. John's, Most Reverend P. J. Skinner, and the General Council of the Sisters of Mercy saw the necessity of acting quickly. Among a number of potential candidates, one young sister stood out above the rest.

Sr. M. Fabian Hennebury had recently returned from studying at the University of Toronto to resume her duties as supervisor of the pediatric department of the hospital. Before coming to any decision, the archbishop and the General Council took a long, hard look at Sr. M. Fabian's qualifications and aptitude for such an important position.

Sr. M. Fabian Hennebury was born in the historic town of Bonavista, the traditional landing place of John Cabot. At her baptism, she was named Mary, which was also her mother's name. Her mother died when she was just nine years of age and, as the oldest girl in a family of eight children—the youngest just seven months old—Mary learned how to accept responsibility at an early age. When she was sixteen, she went as a student to St. Bride's College, Littledale, and during her two years at boarding school, Mary Hennebury began to think about the religious life. She saw that the sisters who taught her were happy, contented women, who had dedicated their lives to helping others through a variety of ministries. Consequently, at the age of nineteen, Mary asked to be accepted as a postulant at Littledale. On July 16, 1936, Mary Hennebury was received into the novitiate and, from that time on, she was known by her religious name, Mary Fabian. After her profession in 1938, Sr. M. Fabian spent a year teaching before she entered St. Clare's school of nursing in 1939, graduating in 1942. A year later, she was sent for postgraduate work at the Toronto Hospital for Sick Children. On her return to St. Clare's, she was appointed supervisor of the pediatric department in the hospital and instructor in pediatrics at the school of nursing.

In 1954, Sr. M. Fabian was asked to move to nursing education. Although she loved her work in pediatrics and had no desire to return to teaching, Sr. M. Fabian accepted the decision of her superiors and enrolled as a student at the University of Toronto. She completed the prescribed courses, received her certificate in nursing education and was looking forward to another year's study to fulfill the requirements for the degree of bachelor of science in nursing when word came from the General Council of the Sisters of Mercy asking her to return to her former position as supervisor of pediatrics. Several other sisters had expressed a keen interest in nursing education, but it was not easy to find someone with Sr. M. Fabian's qualifications and experience in pediatrics! Sr. M. Fabian was by no means disappointed with this decision, in fact, she was elated. She much preferred nursing in the pediatric unit to teaching in the school of nursing, and so, in 1955, she returned to her first love—caring for sick children.

Shortly after her return to St. Clare's, Sr. M. Fabian was asked to enroll in a two-year correspondence course in hospital organization and management offered by the Canadian Hospital Association (CHA). It did not take a genius to guess what the superiors of the Mercy congregation had in mind for Sr. M. Fabian Hennebury. Early in 1955, she was appointed administrator of St. Clare's Mercy Hospital, a position she was to fill for twenty-six years. Her appointment marked a new beginning and a period of unprecedented growth for the hospital.

In spite of her heavy responsibilities as administrator, Sr. M. Fabian kept on studying. She realized that the delivery of health care was a field that was undergoing rapid change. She wanted to be prepared and knowledgeable. So she examined the courses offered at different universities in Canada. She discovered that, at the time, there was no degree program in hospital administration offered in any Canadian university. The only courses available were offered by correspondence. Dutifully, Sr. M. Fabian filled out the necessary forms, materials arrived, and—after a long day in the hospital—she sat at her desk and studied long into the night. Having received her certificate from the CHA, Sr. M. Fabian enrolled in a similar program with the American Hospital Association (AHA). After completing written and oral examinations in Chicago, she was admitted as a member of the association and later qualified for a fellowship from the same association.

Sr. M. Fabian continued to be a member of both the Canadian and American health associations and was active in the AHA as a regent and examiner for the American college for over sixteen years.

Even before she had assumed the position of administrator, Sr. M. Fabian realized the need for formal organization of the medical staff and the establishment of a board of governors for the hospital. After her appointment, one of the first items on her agenda was to meet with the superior general of the Sisters of Mercy, Sr. M. Imelda Smith, and the archbishop to discuss these matters. Both Sr. M. Imelda and Archbishop Skinner were in complete agreement, and on March 15, 1956, the newly formed Board of Governors of St. Clare's Mercy Hospital held its first meeting.[3] From that time up until April 1995, the board of governors met regularly and provided wise direction for the hospital.

The period between 1960 and 2000 saw rapid changes in the delivery of health care in Newfoundland. Technological advances, increasing costs, and the demand for new and better equipment required a dedicated and knowledgeable board of governors for the hospital. Through the years, members of the successive boards of St. Clare's guided the hospital through the difficult years of development and growth. It is largely due to the expertise and dedication of the women and men who were members of the board that St. Clare's Mercy Hospital has taken its place as one of the main centres of health care in Newfoundland.[4]

---

3. Members of the first Board of Governors of St. Clare's Mercy Hospital were: Archbishop P. J. Skinner (chairman); Sr. M. Imelda Smith (superior general of the Sisters of Mercy); Monsignor H. A. Summers, Honourable Robert S. Furlong; Sr. M. Loretta McIsaac; Dr. E. L. Sharpe; Sr. M. Fabian Hennebury (administrator); and Sr. M. Xaverius Kenny (secretary).

4. Appendix B lists the names of the women and men who served on the Board of Directors of St. Clare's Mercy Hospital (1939–1940) and the Board of Governors of St. Clare's Mercy Hospital (1956–1995).

One of the first matters to come to the attention of the new board of governors was the need for a more formal organization of the medical staff. During the first meeting of the board, the administrator of the hospital, Sr. M. Fabian Hennebury, stressed the urgency of having a medical advisory committee. Consequently, in May 1956, the board appointed five members of the medical staff to this committee. Dr. J. B. Murphy became the first president; Dr. G. M. Brownrigg, vice-president; and Dr. R. J. Simms, secretary. Other members of the committee were Dr. T. G. Anderson and Dr. F. L. O'Dea. Over the years, members of the medical advisory committee changed, but one name stands out— that of Dr. Garrett M. Brownrigg. Dr. Brownrigg's vision and foresight was the leading force behind the agreement between the medical school at Memorial University and the board of governors that saw St. Clare's accredited as a teaching hospital.

Shortly after its formation, the newly appointed executive of the medical staff brought to the attention of the board of governors the importance of the accurate preservation of medical records. As a result, Sr. M. Brenda Lacey, a registered nurse who had been on the staff of St. Clare's for several years, was sent to the Halifax Infirmary where she enrolled in a course for medical records librarians. After her graduation in 1957, she was appointed director of the medical records department at St. Clare's, a post she held until her retirement in the fall of 1989. It should be noted here that the term "retirement" is used loosely when applied to a Sister of Mercy.[5] In Sr. M. Brenda's case, she moved from medical records to the general office of the Sisters of Mercy.

With the appointment of the new, dynamic, and visionary

---

5. Some sisters claim that the term "recycled" more aptly describes a member of the congregation who no longer occupies a salaried position. Some sisters have been recycled four or five times, engaged in different ministries as the need arises.

administrator, Sr. M. Fabian Hennebury, the establishment of an active board of governors, and the formation of the medical advisory committee, the financial administration of St. Clare's underwent a thorough reorganization. Liability insurance was taken out for the first time in October 1956. Then, to prepare for the introduction of the National Health Insurance Program, a new accounting system was put in place in January 1957.[6]

At this time, too, the importance of accreditation was being discussed. Because of the inadequate system of keeping medical records that had been in place prior to Sr. M. Brenda Lacey's appointment and the lack of formal organization, the board of governors realized that St. Clare's was not ready to meet the standards required for full accreditation. Nevertheless, it was decided to apply to the Joint Commission on Hospital Accreditation for a preliminary survey to identify deficiencies and suggest improvements. This survey was completed in July 1958, and St. Clare's was given a one-year accreditation with recommendations. So carefully were these recommendations implemented that the following year the hospital was given full accreditation for three years, a status that was maintained as long as St. Clare's remained an independent hospital.

With the introduction of the National Health Insurance Program in 1958, the sisters on the staff of St. Clare's received salaries according to their qualifications and length of service. But even though these salaries were recorded, the sisters did not take them. Instead the sisters' salaries were put into an account and used for the needs of the hospital. Because the loan for the new (1939) hospital on LeMarchant Road had been paid in full, St. Clare's was in a position to

---

6. The Canadian National Health Insurance Program came into effect on July 1, 1958. Canada's National Health Insurance Program, often referred to as "Medicare," is designed to ensure that all residents have reasonable access to medically necessary hospital and physician services on a prepaid basis.

consider further expansion. In April 1959, the announcement was made that a new wing would be added to St. Clare's
that would provide additional facilities for obstetrics, pediatrics, emergency services, and a new dietary department.
Financial arrangements were made for a bank loan to cover
approximately sixty percent of the cost, the remainder being
obtained through federal-provincial grants. Within a compar-
atively short time, this loan, too, was fully repaid by taking five
thousand dollars monthly from the sisters' salaries and
through income from the private room differential.[7]

Prior to the completion of the new wing on St. Clare
Avenue, another important step was taken in 1960 when St.
Clare's Mercy Hospital was incorporated. The act of incorporation gave St. Clare's a legal state of existence and a recognized
corporate identity authorized to operate according to the
approved articles of incorporation. The act gave the archbishop
of St. John's and the superior general of the Sisters of Mercy the
right to appoint members of the board of governors. This provided the Mercy congregation with the means of ensuring that its
mission, philosophy, and values were sustained at the hospital.

The new seven-storey extension made of brick on St.
Clare Avenue was opened on January 8, 1962. While the construction of this extension supported Newfoundland industry,
it caused problems for many years because of leaks that were
major and frequent. Eventually, the structural problems were
corrected, but not without additional expense.

When the dietary department was opened in the new
wing, a central service was introduced. In order to prepare for
this, Sr. M. Andrea Sutton visited St. Joseph's Hospital in Saint
John, New Brunswick, where this system had been in operation for a few years. However, even with the experience and
advice gained at St. Joseph's Hospital, the change from a
decentralized service to a centralized one was difficult. The

---

7. Hennebury, "St. Clare's," ASMSJ, 41.

current wages for dietary personnel at this time were so low that it was impossible to hire competent management or cooks. The decision was made to place the dietary department under contract with V. S. Services.

In June 1967, Sr. M. Aidan Howell, the laboratory supervisor, spearheaded the formation of the St. Clare's Mercy Hospital Auxiliary. Sr. M. Aidan was truly loved and respected by her colleagues in health care and by her sisters in community. Born in Northern Bay, Newfoundland, she received her early education in the Catholic school in her hometown before going to St. Bride's College, Littledale, where she made her decision to enter the Congregation of the Sisters of Mercy. Shortly after her profession in 1942, she enrolled in the school of nursing at St. Clare's, graduating as a nurse in 1945. Subsequently, she attended the University of Toronto where she obtained a degree in laboratory technique. Within a few years, she was appointed supervisor of laboratory services where her sense of humour and her optimistic outlook on life made St. Clare's lab the most popular department in the hospital. Timorous individuals who visited her laboratory to be poked and prodded with needles of all sizes and shapes, emerged from the ordeal with smiling faces!

In 1971, while studying for a master's degree in Baltimore, Sr. M. Aidan became very ill. Immediate surgery was required, and it was discovered that she was suffering from terminal cancer. The sisters in Newfoundland, and particularly her colleagues at St. Clare's, were shocked at this unexpected news. Immediately on receiving the report, Sr. M. St. Clare Maddigan, one of the nurses on the staff of St. Clare's, left for Baltimore to be with Sr. M. Aidan at this difficult time. Naturally, Sr. M. Aidan was anxious to return to St. John's, but her condition was such that the American commercial airlines could not accommodate her. The administrator of Mercy Hospital in Baltimore had a brother who was a high-ranking officer in the United States Army. He obtained transportation for the sisters on a medically equipped army plane that was enroute to Goose Bay, Labrador. It was arranged that the plane would stop at Gander where they could connect with the regular Air Canada flight to St. John's. Sr. M. Aidan died a few weeks later on January 12, 1972. The organization that she established, the St. Clare's Mercy Hospital Auxiliary, continued under the leadership of Sr. M. Mark Hennebury, and within fourteen years of its establishment, it had donated more than $350,000 to the hospital. These and similar contributions allowed the hospital to meet the demands of new technology that required sophisticated, expensive equipment. Over the years, the St. Clare's Mercy Hospital Auxiliary has provided a valuable service to St. Clare's through the operation of the gift shop. In addition, for many years the auxiliary organized a highly successful "Fall Fair" that raised money to supply the hospital with much needed equipment.

In 1966, discussion with Memorial University began that eventually saw St. Clare's recognized as a teaching hospital. The minutes of a meeting of the board of governors on June 30, 1966, record a meeting with the acting president of Memorial University:

The Board met with Dean Morgan, Acting President of MUN, to discuss the proposed plan of the University to open a Medical school on the campus. In the event that this came to pass, Dr. Morgan was interested in the possibility of existing hospitals participating in the teaching program; and the need for coordination of the University Medical School with the hospitals. Dr. Ian Rusted of the University, and Dr. G. Brownrigg the Chief of the Medical staff at St. Clare's were present. Archbishop Skinner expressed his support for these initiatives. He added that St. Clare's was looked upon by a large segment of the population, both in St. John's, and throughout the province, as their medical centre, and that every necessary step would be taken to maintain this role and upgrade facilities as much as possible.[8]

Discussions continued throughout 1967, and in 1968, a formal affiliation agreement was signed with the Memorial University's medical school.[9] In-service education was initiated, and conferences on various topics were held on a biweekly basis. Since that time, St. Clare's has provided clinical teaching and experience to students, interns, and residents in the various medical disciplines.

Needless to say, the new initiatives taking place at St. Clare's placed an almost impossible workload on the administrator, Sr. M. Fabian Hennebury. The problem was brought to the attention of the board and the need for an assistant administrator was discussed. At a board meeting on February 24, 1967, Sr. M. Lucy Power, who was the operating room supervisor, was appointed as Sr. M. Fabian's assistant, to take up her duties in September of that year. Sr. M. Audrey Tobin replaced Sr. M. Lucy in the operating room.

Things were changing rapidly within the health care system in St. John's. Reluctantly, the administrator of St. Clare's, Sr. M. Fabian Hennebury, agreed to the phase-out of the department of pediatrics at the hospital. She realized that the new Dr. Charles A. Janeway Child Health Centre was better prepared to care for children, and furthermore, the city's best pediatricians were attached to the staff of the Janeway. It was a sad day for Sr. M. Fabian when the children at St. Clare's were transferred to the Janeway in 1970. Pediatrics had been her first love, and even in the midst of

---

8. Minutes, BOGSC, June 30, 1966, ASMSJ.

9. Dr. Garrett Brownrigg represented the board of governors of St. Clare's throughout these negotiations.

her busy day as administrator, Sr. M. Fabian always found time to visit the little ones in the pediatric unit.

Over the years, additions and expansions to St. Clare's had been made to take care of immediate needs. In spite of all the new initiatives, the far-sighted administrator was concerned that there was, as yet, no long-term plan for the future of St. Clare's. Sr. M. Fabian brought her concerns to the board of governors, and as a result, in 1966, a hospital consultant firm from Toronto was engaged to complete a survey of the hospital and the acute-care needs for the city. In June 1966, an architect, Mrs. Doris Lojahn, from Agnew, Peckham, and Associates, visited the hospital. She recommended changes in and enlargement of every department of the hospital. In short, these recommendations pointed to the necessity of a large extension to the buildings that already comprised St. Clare's Mercy Hospital.[10] The board decided to apply to the provincial government for a grant that would help defray the cost of such an expansion.

At a meeting of the board of governors on July 29, 1966, Monsignor Harold Summers reported that he had met with the minister of health, Dr. James McGrath, to discuss the proposed extension to the hospital. Dr. McGrath informed Monsignor Summers that the premier (Honourable Joseph R. Smallwood) had approved the expansion project for St. Clare's but that the government was not in a position to provide any grant for the year 1966–1967. However, a week after this interview, Premier Smallwood made a public announcement of hospital expansion. Included in the arrangement—according to the premier—was the project at St. Clare's that would cost between eight and ten million dollars.[11] Wisely, the board directed Monsignor Summers to write Dr. McGrath and request that the premier's statement relating to the expansion to St. Clare's be confirmed in writing. At this same meeting, the far-sighted superior general

10. Minutes, BOGSC, June 6, 1966, ASMSJ.
11. Minutes, BOGSC, July 29, 1966, ASMSJ.

of the Sisters of Mercy, Sr. M. Assumpta Veitch, noted that in light of the imminent expansion of the hospital, it would be necessary to begin purchasing properties adjoining St. Clare's. She agreed that the Mercy congregation would be prepared to cover the interest on the bank loan involved in the purchase of property. The board agreed that this money would be repaid to the Sisters of Mercy when the government grant was obtained.[12] From that point on, the board of governors began to purchase properties adjacent to St. Clare's to prepare the way for the inevitable expansion.

On March 16, 1967, a letter from Dr. J. McGrath, minister of health, confirmed government approval for the erection of a new extension to St. Clare's, although a government grant would not be available until 1968. This cleared the way for the board to announce publicly that in the following year (1968) construction of the new extension to St. Clare's would begin. The plans for expansion included a complete renovation of the 1960–1962 building on St. Clare Avenue.

The first problem encountered in planning extensions to the existing hospital was the site itself. The older buildings were crowded into the corner of a triangle with heavily travelled streets on both sides. In addition, the City of St. John's was planning to build a street through the middle of the available land (now Ricketts Road). The site, however, had one great advantage—the difference in elevation between LeMarchant Road and St. Clare Avenue. Entrances to the building could be provided on three different levels: stores and equipment would be brought in through the basement entrance; food deliveries and garbage removal would use the first floor; and staff and visitors would enter by the entrance on the second floor. Also, there would be a separate emergency entrance and another one for outpatients.

Even though the construction period experienced strikes in every trade, the building was completed in April 1972. At

---

12. Ibid.

that time, the switchboard was changed to its new location and the laboratory staff moved from the crowded quarters in the original hospital, the "White House," to the spacious new facilities. The extension and the renovated 1962 wing of the hospital provided accommodations for three hundred patients, as well as completely new and modern facilities for operating and emergency suites, coronary and intensive care units, diagnostic imaging, newborn and intensive care nurseries, psychiatry, and storage.

The project was completed in 1972, just fifty years after the opening of the first St. Clare's Mercy Hospital.

THE DREAM FULFILLED

The lofty oak from a small acorn grows.
                    —Lewis Duncombe, *De Minimus Maxima*

When St. Clare's Mercy Hospital was blessed and formally opened on May 21, 1922, Archbishop Roche expressed his hopes for the future growth of the institution:

> They [the Sisters of Mercy] are beginning in a very humble way, a philanthropic work which has vast possibilities for good; they are planting a tiny grain of mustard seed, which we hope will grow into an immense tree, throwing its healing branches over different sections of the country.[1]

Then, on October 29, 1939, when the new extension to St. Clare's Mercy Hospital was opened, the archbishop reflected:

> Today, after seventeen years, we are assembled in this splendid new Hospital to see the completion of the work which was then begun . . . Verily, my dear Sisters, the acorn has developed into a mighty oak; the tiny grain of mustard seed has grown, as we hoped it would into a mighty tree.[2]

One wonders if this visionary archbishop could have foreseen

---

1. Archbishop E. P. Roche, Address given at the opening of the 1922 St. Clare's Mercy Hospital, St. John's, May 21, 1922, quoted in Hennebury, "St. Clare's," ASMSJ, 5.

2. Archbishop E. P. Roche, Address given at the opening of St. Clare's Mercy Hospital, St. John's, October 29, 1939, RG 10/9/62, ASMSJ.

that "the work" was not yet complete—that the "mighty tree" was destined for still greater growth.

On September 7, 1972, Mass was offered by Archbishop P. J. Skinner in the St. Clare's chapel to invoke God's blessing on the new extension to St. Clare's Mercy Hospital. All the hospital personnel were invited to attend. This was the first in a series of events that took place to celebrate the opening of the new wing. The official opening of the extension took place September 8, 1972. Invited guests included officials of church and state and civic leaders; representatives of the Sisters of Mercy; Sr. M. Bernard Gladney, the first administrator of St. Clare's; the sisters from St. Clare's Convent; the medical advisory committee; the hospital auxiliary; the medical staff and their wives; and the clergy. The celebrations concluded on September 9. Sisters from all the convents in the city and nearby places and the nursing and paramedical staff from all the city hospitals were given a tour of the hospital. In true Mercy hospitality, a cup of tea was served to all visitors.

The new St. Clare's was a state-of-the-art, modern hospital, the whole complex providing accommodation for 375 patients. The most up-to-date equipment was provided in every department of the hospital. When writing an account of this ambitious project, Sr. M. Fabian acknowledged the invaluable assistance of Monsignor Harold Summers:

Over this difficult period, Msgr. Harold A. Summers . . . gave much of his time and effort to the various projects. As Chairman of the Finance Committee, he took responsibility for the financial planning which he outlined in detail for the Hospital. His schedules covered the whole period for repayment of loans and as a result, payments of interest and principal were always on the date noted. Monsignor retired shortly after arrangements were finished for the Service

Wing, but he maintained an interest in its progress. The Sisters of Mercy will always be grateful for his assistance.[3]

Much of the money for the expansion of the hospital came from the personal sacrifices of the Sisters of Mercy in Newfoundland, who, in order to support St. Clare's and other ministries of the Mercy congregation, lived on a very small percentage of their salaries. In addition, grateful patients, as well as relatives and friends of the sisters, made bequests to St. Clare's. The almost continual changes and renovations carried out in the hospital to meet changing needs were funded, for the most part, from St. Clare's funds and from the Congregation of the Sisters of Mercy rather than from government grants. Many items of major equipment were obtained without government funding. Some of this equipment was purchased from funds donated by the Sisters of Mercy and the St. Clare's Mercy Hospital Auxiliary.

With the completion of the new hospital and the transfer of the laboratory and medical records from the original hospital—the "White House"—the sisters at St. Clare's Convent could at last avail of adequate living space. Up to this time, they had shared the building with the hospital, and the inconvenience and discomfort of such an arrangement are obvious. Nevertheless, for fifty years, the sisters at St. Clare's had coped uncomplainingly with this situation, most of them using small rooms in the attic as their bedrooms. Only the most senior among them warranted a room on the second floor!

In the meantime, the Department of Health was planning to close the Tuberculosis Sanatorium on Topsail Road. The government turned to St. Clare's with the request that the hospital open a unit for patients suffering from tuberculosis. The hospital agreed, and in May 1973, patients were transferred

3. Hennebury, "St. Clare's," ASMSJ, 45–46.

from the Sanatorium to the second, third, and fourth floors of St. Clare's. Within a year, it became clear that twenty beds would be adequate for the tuberculosis-chest patients, and the fourth floor of the 1939 hospital was renovated for this purpose. This encouraged the government to make a further request. Could St. Clare's provide a thirty-bed unit for convalescent orthopedic patients who were to be moved when the new General Hospital was constructed? Once more the board of governors at St. Clare's agreed to cooperate, and the second and third floors of the 1939 building were renovated for convalescent orthopedic patients from the General Hospital as well as from St. Clare's acute-care units.

As new and more effective treatments for tuberculosis became available, the incidence of the illness dropped significantly. Consequently, admission to St. Clare's for treatment of the disease continued to decrease. The hospital decided to install ultraviolet light in all rooms on Fourth Floor South so that patients with others forms of chest problems, such as emphysema and carcinoma, could be admitted there for investigation and therapy. A year or so later, at the request of the Department of Health, the tuberculosis clinic on Harvey Road was transferred to St. Clare's. Approximately 250 patients with tuberculosis were treated at any one time at this clinic. As well, the clinic continued routine pre-employment X-rays and follow-up X-rays on patients who had contact with tuberculosis.

St. Clare's Mercy Hospital, of course, has always been concerned for the needs of the whole person, physical, emotional, and spiritual. Since the small beginnings of the hospital in 1922, pastoral care was always part of the ministry of St. Clare's, although not in a formally organized manner. As understood at St. Clare's, pastoral care is a ministry of compassion dedicated to meeting the spiritual needs of patients and families. On September 18, 1975, the pastoral care department was formally established at St. Clare's under the direction of Sr.

M. Carmelita Power, who had recently completed a master's degree in this discipline.[4] Her first assistant was Sr. M. Placide Conway. Throughout the years since that time, a number of Sisters of Mercy have served in this department at St. Clare's. The purpose of the department is to coordinate services for the various religions and to make sure they are available to all patients. It also includes staff education.

In the history of St. Clare's Mercy Hospital, it seems that there was no standing still. No sooner than one new department was established and off and running, new needs presented themselves. Throughout her years as a nurse and especially in her role as administrator, Sr. M. Fabian Hennebury was aware of the helplessness of many men and women who were trying to fight an addiction to alcohol. When, in 1977, the provincial government requested that St. Clare's administer a detoxification centre, to be financed by the government, the request met with Sr. M. Fabian's wholehearted approval. She brought the matter to St. Clare's board of governors, who supported her proposal to initiate plans for the centre.[5] However, although the government had agreed to finance the project, it seemed that they expected St. Clare's to provide the site for such a centre. Once more, the Congregation of the Sisters of Mercy came to the rescue. An ideal location was found on Deanery Avenue in downtown St. John's. The building, owned by St. Patrick's Parish, had been formerly used as a school operated by the Presentation Sisters. The Sisters of Mercy purchased the building from St. Patrick's Parish and turned it over to St. Clare's Mercy Hospital. With the help of the federal government, the building was renovated to make it suitable for its new purpose. On May 1, 1978, the facility known as Talbot House was blessed and opened by the chairman of the St. Clare's board, Monsignor David Morrissey.

Talbot House was a non-medical residential facility that

4. Minutes, BOGSC, September 18, 1975, ASMSJ.
5. Minutes, BOGSC, October 25, 1976, ASMSJ.

provided a quiet, unthreatening refuge for people needing help when intoxicated.[6] In addition to providing the detoxification centre, St. Clare's offered treatment for the alcoholic, both in the psychiatric in-patient unit and in the day-care program. Self-help programs were offered at Talbot House, and through this centre, St. Clare's Mercy Hospital continued for many years to offer sanctuary to people fighting the disease of alcoholism.

Initially, Talbot House operated under the direction of the Board of Governors of St. Clare's Mercy Hospital and was funded by the Department of Social Services. However, in 1982, the operating budget for Talbot House was provided through the Alcohol and Drug Dependency Commission (ADDC). This arrangement continued until 1990 when, on March 22, 1990, Archbishop A. L. Penney of St. John's and Aidan Maloney, chairman of St. Clare's Mercy Hospital board of governors, issued the following joint statement:

Effective April 1, 1990, Talbot House Detoxification Centre will be administered by the Alcohol and Drug Dependency Commission (ADDC) of Newfoundland and Labrador . . . This initiative will not have any adverse impact on the day-to-day operation of Talbot house. It is intended to ensure that essential treatment services are provided as effectively as possible and that fragmentation of effort is minimized . . . St. Clare's is strongly committed to addictions treatment and rehabilitation. As part of this commitment, St. Clare's will continue to provide Talbot House with various support services and medical back-up as required.[7]

---

6. Hennebury, "St. Clare's," ASMSJ, 48.

7. "Talbot House to Be Administered by the ADDC of Newfoundland and Labrador," *Evening Telegram*, March 22, 1990, 3. Talbot House was replaced in 1999 by a new detoxification centre called the Recovery Centre in the area of St. John's known as Pleasantville. This centre, in addition to providing a residential facility for people needing shelter when intoxicated, provides educational and treatment programs.

Another area of health care in which St. Clare's led the way was the care of the terminally ill. As far back as 1975, the plight of persons suffering from terminal illness was brought to the attention of the board of governors. The long-range planning committee brought forward a plan for a palliative care unit for terminal care similar to that at the Royal Victoria Hospital in Montreal.[8] Up to this time, no such facility existed in Newfoundland. The board gave cautious approval but suggested that a lot more study had to be done. The establishment of such a department at the hospital would need a specially trained staff and a good deal of financing. The planning committee went back to the drawing board and, in October of the following year, came back with the following statement:

> The committee sees as a priority area the need for a pallia-
> tive care unit which should be designed to care for those
> who are terminally ill. The planning for this department
> will take some time and a sub-committee of the Long
> Range [sic] Planning Committee will strive to do this
> planning. Sr. M. Fabian agreed to chair this committee.[9]

The planning committee met often and consulted wide-ly. In June 1977, a meeting of a joint committee of the board and the planning committee took place. Sr. M. Fabian informed the committee that, at a recent meeting with government, the proposal to establish a palliative care unit at St. Clare's had been approved in principle and that the hospital had been invited to prepare a detailed budget for considera-tion. Sr. Fabian was encouraged that Dr. Wallace Ingram, one of the senior doctors on the staff, had expressed keen

---

8. Minutes, BOGSC, June 26, 1975, ASMSJ.
9. Minutes, BOGSC, October 28, 1976, ASMSJ.

interest in the unit.[10] Dr. Ingram recommended that one or two staff members should, if possible, visit St. Christopher's Hospice in London, England. Further encouragement for this move came from the Royal Victoria Hospital that offered to train one member of the nursing staff for a period of a month and also to send their own head nurse to help organize the unit as soon as it was opened.[11]

However, there were still major obstacles in the way of establishing a palliative care unit at St. Clare's. Although the Newfoundland government approved in principle the establishment of such a facility at St. Clare's, government was not in a position to provide funding. But, at the same time, the idea was supported by the Health Insurance Division of the Department of Health, and Mr. Hearn, the assistant deputy minister of health, suggested that St. Clare's proceed with planning the groundwork for the project.[12]

And so time passed. The committee worked tirelessly on the problem of funding. Finally, in September 1979, the board was informed that the government had agreed to partial funding of the unit for the following six months. Newfoundland's Medical Care Plan (MCP) had agreed to pay a physician. Because of the staffing pattern, the narcotics bureau agreed to waive its legislation requiring two signatures for all narcotics and to accept the signature of one registered nurse. Through the hard work of the planning committee, and a large donation by the Congregation of the Sisters of Mercy, the unit was ready

---

10. In 1998, Dr. Ingram won the Atlantic Provinces Regional Award for outstanding service, given by the Royal College of Physicians and Surgeons of Canada. He was chosen for this award by the regional advisory committee, a group of specialty physicians in the Atlantic provinces. In 2007, Dr. Ingram was honoured by the Canadian Society of Internal Medicine with a CSIM Osler Award.

11. Minutes, joint committee of the board of governors and the long-range planning committee, St. Clare's Mercy Hospital, June 8, 1977, ASMSJ.

12. Minutes, BOGSC, June 29, 1978, ASMSJ.

to open on October 1, 1979. It was the first facility of this nature to be established in the Atlantic provinces.[13] There was a good deal of publicity surrounding the opening of the palliative care unit, for the board of governors was anxious the hospital provide the public with accurate information regarding the purpose of the unit, lest it be perceived as a "death ward." Sr. M. Fabian described the role of the palliative care unit as follows:

> In order to assist them [the patients and their families] at this time, we believe in total supportive care of the patient, by our reverence for life—not necessarily prolonging terminal illness, but by assisting the terminally ill patient to live fully, to preserve mental alertness and to experience the support of family and a caring community. There are two main goals for this unit:
>
> 1) To maintain a family oriented program apart from the acute care hospital setting, and
>
> 2) To free the patient from pain and its associated mental anguish and anxiety by a program of pain control.[14]

The response to the unit was very positive, and within days of its opening, a large number of volunteers offered their services. In addition to providing financial aid, the Sisters of Mercy provided two sisters for ministry in the palliative care unit, one in pastoral care and the second in nursing. Donations poured in from the public, as well as from members of the staff of St. Clare's. Nevertheless, it should not be forgotten that it was through the compassion and vision of Sr. M. Fabian Hennebury, and with the financial assistance of the Sisters of Mercy, that palliative care first became a reality in this province.

Over the years, the palliative care unit at St. Clare's has

---

13. Minutes, BOGSC, September 27, 1977, ASMSJ.
14. Hennebury, "St. Clare's," ASMSJ, 49.

given comfort and hope to thousands of people during their darkest hours. Not only were the sick relieved of much suffering, but also the pain of relatives and friends was alleviated by the loving concern of medical staff and volunteers especially trained for this ministry. It is one of the ironies of life that the first Sister of Mercy to die in the palliative care unit was Sr. M. Fabian's younger sister, Sr. M. Mark Hennebury, who died of cancer on January 14, 1984. Sr. M. Mark was a registered nurse who spent most of her religious life caring for the sick. With the exception of six years when she was administrator of St. Patrick's Mercy Home, she lived and worked at St. Clare's. All those who worked with her, especially members of the St. Clare's auxiliary, remember Sr. M. Mark with affection and gratitude. The sisters in St. Clare's Convent recall her matter-of-fact attitude toward an illness that she accepted with uncomplaining patience. She continued her work with the auxiliary until one day she announced quietly to the sisters that it was time for her to move to the palliative care unit. She died the next day.

The period from 1955 to 1982 was a time when St. Clare's Mercy Hospital knew phenomenal growth, not only in the size of the physical plant, in the services offered, and in its outreach programs, but especially in the qualifications, expertise, and reputation of the people who staffed the hospital. This period coincided with M. Fabian Hennebury's tenure as administrator of the hospital. Her constant aim was to maintain the position of St. Clare's as a general hospital with the highest accreditation. For her progressive stance and her contributions to health care, she received national and international recognition. Included in her many awards was the Order of Canada, which was presented to her on December 17, 1984, in recognition of her outstanding achievement in service to humanity.

Of course, M. Fabian Hennebury did not work alone. With the establishment of the Board of Governors of St.

Clare's Mercy Hospital in 1956, Sr. M. Fabian worked with a group of experienced and knowledgeable people who developed wise policies that established the future direction of the hospital. She had the advice, co-operation, and dedication of the sisters and staff of St. Clare's Mercy Hospital, the support and encouragement of successive General Councils of the Sisters of Mercy, and the confidence of the archbishop and administration board of the Archdiocese of St. John's. Furthermore, it must be recorded that throughout her tenure as executive director, Sr. M. Fabian established at St. Clare's a standard of excellence in the delivery of care that was a model for her successors. M. Fabian retired from St. Clare's in 1981.

At a meeting of the board of governors on December 17, 1981, Sr. M. Lucy Power was nominated as the new executive director of St. Clare's. Sr. M. Lucy, who had been the assistant administrator of the hospital for several years, continued to implement the far-sighted policies of her predecessor and of the board of governors. In 1982, Sr. M. Lucy Power requested and received a dispensation from her religious vows and, a short time later, married Patrick Dobbin. However, Lucy Dobbin remained as executive director of St. Clare's until 1986.

The difficult financial position of the Newfoundland government during the 1980's required severe cutbacks in all areas of public services. The hospitals, of course, were not exempt. At the same time, the need for new modern equipment was an ongoing concern. For this reason, the board of governors of St. Clare's looked into the feasibility of establishing the St. Clare's Mercy Hospital Foundation. The purpose of the foundation was to raise money to purchase the most up-to-date equipment for the various departments of the hospital. The foundation began its work in the fall of 1984 under the chairmanship of Mr. Aidan Maloney. One of the first campaigns initiated by St. Clare's Mercy Hospital Foundation was launched in December 1985. The object was to raise money to renew and replace equipment. The campaign was successfully concluded on the scheduled date, August 11, 1986, with its goal exceeded by almost two hundred thousand dollars.[15] In the years that followed, the foundation was very effective in raising millions of dollars to allow the hospital to fund special projects and to purchase new and expensive equipment.

In 1984, St. Clare's was chosen to be one of the ten national test sites for a management information system project. The following year, in 1985, St. Clare's laboratory had the distinction of becoming the first computerized laboratory in Newfoundland and Labrador and one of the first in Canada. The laboratory was fully accredited and participated in the training of laboratory personnel with the Memorial University of Newfoundland medical school and the Cabot College of Applied Arts, Technology and Continuing Education.

Already in the 1970s such innovations as prenatal classes, couple participation in labour, sibling visitation, and rooming-in were available at St. Clare's. During the same period, patient education was organized on a more formal basis, and a natural family-planning clinic was established. These initiatives were more fully realized when, in 1985, a family-centred maternity care policy was implemented. This move grew out of awareness that more relevant maternal/child health services were needed in a facility such as St. Clare's that had already broken down many of the traditional barriers in maternal/newborn care. Another factor that influenced this move was the need to improve the practice setting for student nurses who used this clinical facility for the maternal/child health component in an integrated nursing curriculum. This was something new because now the emphasis was placed on nursing the new family, rather than having the nursing student gain experience in the traditional postpartum unit with a central nursery.

---

15. Aidan Maloney, chairman, St. Clare's Mercy Hospital Foundation, Minutes, BOGSC, September 25, 1986, ASMSJ.

In April 1986, St. Clare's assumed responsibility for the administration of the Dr. Walter Templeman Hospital on Bell Island.[16] This was in response to a government policy of placing small hospitals under the administrative structure of larger regional facilities. The executive director of St. Clare's, Lucy Dobbin, explained that these changes involved making available various types of expertise and helped provide medical services that were not readily available on Bell Island. Furthermore, ongoing education and training programs at St. Clare's were extended to personnel at the Bell Island hospital.

Also in 1986, Lucy Dobbin resigned from her position at St. Clare's when she was appointed chief executive officer of the General Hospital at the Health Sciences Complex in St. John's. In June 1986, Sr. Elizabeth Davis succeeded Mrs. Dobbin as executive director at St. Clare's.

When Elizabeth Davis decided to join the Sisters of Mercy in 1966, she looked forward to a future in teaching. After graduating from Memorial University of Newfoundland with a bachelor's degree in arts and education, she decided to study for a master's degree in theology from the University of Notre Dame in Indiana. Meanwhile, she pursued an active career as a teacher in schools administered by the Sisters of Mercy in different parts of Newfoundland. Then, in 1982, she was asked to leave teaching, which she thoroughly enjoyed, and study at the Institute of Religious Formation (IRF) in St. Louis, Missouri, to prepare for the position of director of formation. However, before the end of that academic year, in March 1983, the superior general, Sr. Patricia Maher, asked her to consider administration at St. Clare's Mercy Hospital. Sr. Elizabeth completed the IRF program and, in September 1983, went to the University of Toronto to begin a master's program in

---

16. "St. Clare's Board to Run Hospital on Bell Island," *Evening Telegram*, March 31, 1986, 3.

health science (administration). At the beginning of each of her two years of study in Toronto, she received an Open Masters Fellowship in recognition of previous academic achievement. Then, during the first year of her studies, she was awarded the Foster G. McGaw Medal and Scholarship in recognition of past achievements. As a requirement for the degree, at the conclusion of each academic year, Sr. Elizabeth engaged in a practical experience and received the R. Alan Hay Memorial Prize. She was the first student to receive this award two years in succession. In May 1985, Sr. Elizabeth accepted the Robert Wood Johnson Award, an award that is presented to the graduating student judged by the faculty as the one most likely to contribute valuable service to the health administration discipline. On November 27, 1985, Sr. Elizabeth graduated from the University of Toronto with a master of health science (administration).

On her return to St. John's, Sr. Elizabeth was appointed assistant executive officer of St. Clare's Mercy Hospital, and on June 16, 1986, she became the executive director of St. Clare's. A few days later, a reporter for the *Evening Telegram* wrote:

"Mercy above all" is a long-standing tradition at St. Clare's Mercy Hospital and it will be maintained under the hospital's new executive director, Sister Elizabeth Davis.

The new executive director at St. Clare's has the onerous task of running the 323-bed facility that provides direct health care service of 10,000 in-patients per year. Last year 214,000 persons used the out-patient facilities and another 38,000 were seen in the emergency centre.

St. Clare's boasts the busiest general surgical facility in the province and has the only palliative care unit. In addition to a rheumatic disease unit, it supervises diagnosis and treatment of about 80,000 arthritics and operates a psychiatric program. It is also a major referral for chest surgery and medicine, general orthopedics and reconstructive surgery, obstetrics, and Gynaecology.[17]

Sr. Elizabeth Davis was not long in establishing herself as a capable and compassionate administrator. Less that a year after her appointment, St. Clare's was awarded the highest level of accreditation available for hospitals in Canada.

The Canadian Council on Hospital Accreditation has six levels of accreditation status. The highest level, which has been awarded to St. Clare's is valid for three years and is granted only to institutions which have a compliance standard above the national average.[18]

Because this was the ninth time that St. Clare's had received this award, the Newfoundland hospital was recognized as being consistent in meeting the highest standards of care in all of Canada.

The accreditation level awarded to St. Clare's was not the only mark of recognition received by the hospital in 1986. On February 18, 1986, a headline in the *Evening Telegram* announced in big, bold letters: "St. Clare's Physiotherapy Department Receives Highest Accreditation in Canada."[19]

However, health care in Newfoundland was becoming more and more costly. The cash-strapped Newfoundland government asked the hospitals to consider ways of cutting costs by sharing services. At a meeting of St. Clare's board of governors in September 1986, the new executive director, Sr.

17. Emily Dyckson, "New St. Clare's Executive Director Says: Tradition of Mercy Above All Will Be Maintained at the Hospital," *Evening Telegram*, June 19, 1986, 9.

18. "Highest Form of Accreditation Awarded to St. Clare's Hospital," *Sunday Express*, January 25, 1987, 3.

19. "St. Clare's Physiotherapy Department Receives Highest Accreditation in Canada," Focus Section, *Evening Telegram*, February 18, 1986.

Elizabeth Davis, pointed out three areas that needed to be studied: 1) the identification of new services; 2) a method of sharing the seventeen services that the hospitals identified as having the potential for sharing; and 3) an alternative method for the delivery of health care services. Sr. Elizabeth noted that at the most recent meeting of the St. John's Hospital Council, the possibility was raised of either the Grace General Hospital or St. Clare's becoming the sole maternity hospital in the city. However, at that time St. Clare's was not willing to give up its obstetrics/gynaecology department, nor was it willing to become the sole maternity hospital.[20] Nevertheless, in the months and years that followed, the possibility of losing obstetrics was never far from the minds of the members of the board.

The new executive director of St. Clare's was a woman of broad vision and decisive action. She was not slow in bringing into effect some of the issues that affected society as a whole, one of these being the environment. In November 1987, the task force for energy management, which was under the direction of the Department of Energy, Mines and Resources of Canada, presented St. Clare's with an award for most outstanding achievement in successful energy management in Newfoundland.[21] Then, in March 1989, Sr. Elizabeth requested the approval of the board of governors to establish a fund for assistance to developing countries for health care projects.[22] Thus, the care and concern of St. Clare's Mercy Hospital became international in scope. At the request of the Congregation of the Sisters of Mercy, Sr. Elizabeth visited Peru in December 1989. While she was there, she participated in the opening of a medical clinic sponsored by the Sisters of Mercy of Newfoundland. St. Clare's provided materials for the clinic from its Developing Countries Fund that had been established in March of that year.

---

20. Minutes, BOGSC, September 25, 1986, ASMSJ.
21. Minutes, BOGSC, November 26, 1987, ASMSJ.
22. Minutes, BOGSC, March 2, 1989, ASMSJ.

In January 1989, Mr. Aidan Maloney succeeded Monsignor David P. Morrissey as chairman of the Board of Governors of St. Clare's Mercy Hospital. Mr. Maloney had been a member of the board since 1974 and was the first chairman of the St. Clare's Mercy Hospital Foundation. As the first layperson to chair the board of governors of St. Clare's, Mr. Maloney was to guide the hospital through some the most difficult years of its history.

In May 1989, the financial officer for St. Clare's, Mr. John McGrath, reported that a major upgrade to St. Clare's computer configuration had taken place during the year and that St. Clare's had begun sharing these services with other health care institutions. St. Clare's was well recognized across Canada with regard to its information systems. In the year 1989, personnel from fourteen hospitals visited St. Clare's to view the system in place and what had been accomplished to date. Some of these visitors were from the Royal Columbia Hospital and the Eagle Ridge Hospital both located in Vancouver, the North York General Hospital in Toronto, the Port Arthur General Hospital in Thunder Bay, and the Isaak Walton Killiam Children's Hospital and the Grace General Hospital in Halifax.[23]

As new programs and initiatives were introduced at the hospital, the work of the executive director of St. Clare's was becoming more complex. For this reason, in 1989, in addition to Dr. Sean Conroy, the assistant executive director, Sr. Phyllis Corbett was appointed as a second assistant executive director of nursing and patient care services. Sr. Phyllis had already served as director of nursing for several years before taking on this additional responsibility.

In June 1989, the whole St. Clare's community was shocked and grieved by the tragic death of one of the hospital's employees, Albert Rogers. Albert was a graduate of the work

---

23. St. Clare's Mercy Hospital Annual Report, 1988–1989, ASMSJ.

experience program at Pine Grove School—a school for developmentally delayed children. Albert had been working at St. Clare's for sixteen years and was a universal favourite with staff and patients alike. Albert was struck by a car while riding his bicycle and died of his injuries. He was thirty-two years of age at the time of his death. The following tribute was circulated throughout the hospital at the time of Albert's death:

Albert came to St. Clare's in 1973 and quickly captured the minds and hearts of the total institution. In some ways he had become almost an adopted son whom everyone loved and protected. Albert knew everyone, greeted everyone, and quickly became indispensible. Whenever something had to be done such as delivering flowers or packages, running errands, assisting visitors or patients, he was there. The daily delivery of the newspaper brought Albert to most areas of the hospital and his friendly greetings and conversations were a highlight of the day . . . Who can forget Albert's participation in hospital events, especially in the annual Christmas Concert and the many dances throughout the years! Albert loved life and shared this love with all who met him in the hospital. Without question, he touched the hearts of all who came in contact with him whether patient, staff or visitor. We will all miss Albert and the special joy he brought to our lives.[24]

In a hospital where sickness, pain, and death are encountered on a daily basis, the death of Albert Rogers was felt as a personal loss by each member of the staff. Albert had contributed so much to the spirit of St. Clare's—to putting a human face on an institution—it was unthinkable that his contribution could ever be forgotten. For this reason, the hospital administration established the Albert Rogers Award in his

---

24. St. Clare's Mercy Hospital, "Tribute to Albert Rogers," June 1989, ASMSJ.

memory. The award, established in December 1989, is presented annually to the employee, physician, or volunteer who best demonstrates the spirit of the St. Clare's community as outlined in the hospital's mission statement. The recipient is an employee of St. Clare's Mercy Hospital (including contractual employees), a physician who regularly works at the hospital, or a volunteer who regularly performs volunteer duties. Each employee, physician, or volunteer at St. Clare's is eligible to vote for the person they believe best shows the spirit of St. Clare's. The award is in the form of a plaque with a $100 gift certificate and is presented every year during the month of December. In this way, St. Clare's Mercy Hospital continues to honour the memory of one of the hospital's most loved employees.

All through the years, St. Clare's Mercy Hospital has been a vital part of the ministry of the Congregation of the Sisters of Mercy in Newfoundland. The congregation had been directly involved in the growth and development of the hospital not only through financial support, but also by making it possible for sister-nurses to pursue postgraduate studies so that they would be better qualified to direct the ever-increasing complexity of medical services at the hospital. However, it was not only the physical healing and well-being of the patients that concerned the Sisters of Mercy. They were concerned for the well-being of the whole person, physical, emotional, and spiritual. Also, they felt that it was important to articulate the mission of the hospital. Thus, one of the decisions of the 1989 General Chapter of the Sisters of Mercy was to appoint a director of mission effectiveness at St. Clare's Mercy Hospital. Sr. Madonna Gatherall began this work in September 1990 at the hospital.

After her appointment as director of mission effectiveness, one of the first tasks that Sr. Madonna undertook was to complete the process of revising the mission statement of St.

Clare's which had been initiated the previous year. By 1991, the statement was complete and a ceremony was held in St. Clare's chapel during which the new statement was proclaimed.[25] Representatives of the Sisters of Mercy, the board of governors, the administration, and various departments were present to receive a copy of the statement so that it could be displayed throughout the hospital. The key element of the statement was that St. Clare's is dedicated to the healing ministry of Jesus and the Church, through being faithful to the mission and values of Jesus, and to witness to his spirit, particularly his mercy and compassion.

---

25. See appendix C.

LETTING GO

You have seen the house built . . . it is now dedicated to
God . . . One more light set on a hill . . . And what shall we
say of the future?
—T. S. Eliot

By the year 1990, the government's plan to restructure the
health care system in the province was gaining momentum.
In October 1990, the St. Clare's board retreat held at
Littledale included members of the board of governors, the
medical advisory committee, and senior management of the
hospital. The retreat focused on long-term planning and
specifically on issues related to the proposed government
options concerning the role of acute-care hospitals in St.
John's. At the next meeting of the board, the chairman, Mr.
Aidan Maloney, noted that the retreat was valuable and
informative in light of decisions on centralization/rationaliza-
tion which were likely to be made by the government in the
near future.[1]

For the following two years, Mr. Maloney and Sr.
Elizabeth Davis, the executive director of St. Clare's, kept in
close touch with the minister of health and the deputy ministers so that the board of governors, the medical advisory committee, and the staff of St. Clare's would be well-informed of
the government's evolving plans for health care delivery in the
province. Everyone realized that the cost of health care was

---

1. Minutes, BOGSC, November 15, 1990, ASMSJ.

skyrocketing, and already the government was insisting on a policy of centralization of some services.

One of the first casualties of this policy was the obstetrical unit at St. Clare's. On April 1, 1992, a ceremony of gratitude and farewell was held to mark the transfer of obstetrics and neonatology from St. Clare's to the Grace General Hospital. In her remarks, Sr. Elizabeth Davis expressed gratitude for the lives of the 83,000 babies born at St. Clare's, for the staff who had given such competent and compassionate care to these babies and their mothers, and for the Congregation of the Sisters of Mercy, who, for sixty-eight years, supported this service. In saying farewell, Sr. Elizabeth mentioned the sadness felt by all associated with the hospital at the loss of obstetrics and neonatology, and she asked for God's blessing on the Grace General Hospital, the present staff, the new staff, and the babies who would be born there. The actual transfer of obstetrics from St. Clare's to the Grace Hospital took place on April 7, 1992. On May 3, 1992, one of the local papers carried a headline, "The Stork Doesn't Call Here Any More." The reporter, Moira Baird, explained:

The sign on the fourth floor of St. Clare's Mercy Hospital says OBSTETRICS, but newborn babies and bassinets are nowhere to be seen. These days the floor houses an expanded psychiatric unit.

On April 7, just six weeks away from the hospital's 70th anniversary in May, the St. Clare's obstetrical unit moved down the road to the Grace General Hospital. For St. Clare's, that was the end of an era—one that began in 1922 when the first baby was born in what was then called the "White House" . . . Since that day more than 83,000 babies have been delivered at the hospital and St. Clare's has gone from 20 beds to over 300.[2]

---

2. Moira Baird, "The Stork Doesn't Call Here Any More," *Evening Telegram*, May 3, 1992, 3.

When the announcement was made that St. Clare's was to lose its obstetrical department, Sr. M. Fabian Hennebury, former executive director of the hospital, remarked, "I feel sad about it. There's something about new birth and new life that makes for something positive in an atmosphere of suffering and pain and sadness."[3] In a statement to the press, Sr. Elizabeth Davis, executive director of the hospital, explained, "Our obstetrical unit was occupied maybe 60 percent of the time, as was the Grace. So, we knew the time had come to create one obstetrical unit."[4] But there were other, more serious considerations. The article in the *Evening Telegram* continued:

> According to Sister Fabian Hennebury, these [considerations] included trends in medicine toward sterilization, genetic engineering, and an increasing demand for abortions. This was bound to present an ethical dilemma for St. Clare's if it became the only centre for obstetrics in St. John's.[5]

Sr. Elizabeth agreed, stating in a press release:

> St. Clare's had to consider the possibility of the service being fully centralized at this hospital. The Hospital's owners [the Congregation of the Sisters of Mercy] and the Board of Governors, in consultation with the Archbishop of St. John's, accepted the fact that, given its ethical tradition, St. Clare's could not provide the full scope of services to which the community was entitled. This meant that if the service had to be centralized, it could not be centralized at St. Clare's.[6]

In spite of the great sadness she felt at the loss of obstetrics

---

3. Ibid.
4. Ibid.
5. Ibid.
6. Ibid.

and neonatology, Sr. Elizabeth Davis was not the sort of person to waste time wringing her hands and bewailing her losses when there were so many sick and suffering people needing help. St. Clare's was about to play a dominant role in the government's restructuring plan. On the same day that the obstetrical unit at St. Clare's was transferred to the Grace General Hospital, the twenty-six bed psychiatry ward at the Grace was closed and all the patients transferred to St. Clare's. In addition to taking over mental health services, the role of St. Clare's was enhanced in other areas, such as musculoskeletal diseases, respiratory diseases, gastrointestinal and abdominal disorders, internal medicine, and ambulatory care. All of this needed careful planning and a certain amount of reconstruction of existing facilities within the hospital. Sr. Elizabeth figured that, for the foreseeable future, she would be more than usually busy. She had no idea of just how busy she was going to be.

As if the executive director of St. Clare's did not have enough to occupy her time, early in 1992, *Chatelaine* magazine requested an interview with Sr. Elizabeth. The magazine planned to publish a profile of hospital service in Canada. The interview with Sr. Elizabeth focused mainly on ambulatory care and the leading role of St. Clare's in this area. The article was published in the fall of 1992 and St. Clare's was named as one of the "Twelve Great Canadian Hospitals."[7]

In October 1992, Sr. Elizabeth advised the board of governors that an Award of Merit was presented to the Sisters of Mercy on their 150th anniversary and the 70th anniversary of St. Clare's. The award was in memory of Sr. Mary Aidan Howell, who was a founding member of the Newfoundland Branch of the Canadian Society of Laboratory Technologists.[8]

---

7. Minutes, BOGSC, May 28, 1992, ASMSJ, and Minutes, BOGSC, October 16, 1992, ASMSJ.

8. Minutes, BOGSC, October 16, 1992, ASMSJ.

Earlier in this same year, 1992, the provincial government brought down its annual budget. During the budget speech in the House of Assembly in March 1992, Dr. Hubert Kitchen, minister of health, stated that the government would be looking at ways to reduce the number of hospital boards in the province.[9] Shortly afterwards, the minister of health invited Mrs. Lucy Dobbin to lead an advisory committee to examine the feasibility of implementing the government's plan and to identify ways to more effectively utilize scarce human and fiscal resources.

At a meeting of the St. Clare's board of governors it was noted:

> The proposal [to reduce the number of health boards] as it stands has very serious implications for St. Clare's Mercy Hospital, and the board feels that its autonomy and ownership is threatened by such a move. More and more across the country we are seeing consolidation of hospital boards and as a result the disappearance of religious from the health care system.[10]

The board of governors at St. Clare's acted immediately and drew up a proposal on board restructuring to be presented to Mrs. Dobbin. On September 24, 1992, the executive committee of the board met with Mrs. Dobbin in the boardroom at St. Clare's and presented her with a copy of St. Clare's Mercy Hospital's response to the proposed board restructuring.

In presenting Mrs. Dobbin with this document, the chairman of the board, Mr. Aidan Maloney, noted that the impetus for this discussion arose out of a remark in the 1992 budget speech:

9. Newfoundland and Labrador, Fourth Session of the Forty-First General Assembly of Newfoundland, *House of Assembly Proceedings* 41, no. 24 (April 9, 1992) preliminary report, Hansard, 695, ASMSJ.

10. Minutes, BOGSC, May 28, 1992, ASMSJ.

Mr. Maloney indicated that following this announcement [of the proposed reduction of the number of hospital boards], St. Clare's had met with the Minister of Health, but received no detailed explanation for such a move. He [Mr. Maloney] stressed that St. Clare's Board had adopted an upfront, honest attitude to this proposal and it is our hope that this is reflected in our presentation. The Department of Health appears to be pleased with St. Clare's cooperation in the past and we hope we will be able together to find an acceptable solution to this dilemma.[11]

Sr. Elizabeth pointed out "that one of the most important issues for St. Clare's Mercy Hospital is the issue of the appointment of the Chairman of the Board and of the Executive Director. She [Sr. Elizabeth Davis] noted that the Sisters of Mercy feel very strongly that the mission of the hospital must be preserved."[12]

In the introduction to the proposal presented by St. Clare's Mercy Hospital to Mrs. Lucy Dobbin, the hospital reiterated its commitment to the province's health care system and committed itself to ensuring the optimal use of human and financial resources to provide the best possible health care for the people of this province. Furthermore, it was pointed out that the Board of Governors of St. Clare's Mercy Hospital also represented the perspective of the Dr. Walter Templeman Hospital on Bell Island as provided through input from that hospital's advisory committee.

The proposal to Mrs. Dobbin dealt with five issues of major importance to St. Clare's:

---

11. Minutes, Executive Committee of the Board of Governors of St. Clare's Mercy Hospital, September 24, 1992, ASMSJ.
12. Ibid.

1) the essential links between the ownership and governance of St. Clare's, links which bring added value to both quality and care for patients and responsible stewardship of human and financial resources;

2) the strong record of the board in the governance of St. Clare's;

3) the concerns for both patient care and effective use of resources when there are large, complex board structures;

4) the objectives that are critical to St. Clare's and the Dr. Walter Templeman hospital in any board restructuring;

5) the openness and flexibility of the board in addressing any options for restructuring that respect the objectives of their two hospitals.

The proposal pointed out that the issue of governance and ownership was of great significance to St. Clare's, which was owned by the Congregation of the Sisters of Mercy of Newfoundland and separately incorporated under its Incorporation Act (1960). The proposal stated further that throughout the hospital's seventy year history, the mission and philosophy of St. Clare's have added value to the care provided to the patients without any form of discrimination. Without the right of appointing board members, as guaranteed in the act of incorporation, the Sisters of Mercy feared that they could not carry out their mission and would be faced with the possibility of withdrawing from ownership of the hospital. If this were to happen, it would have serious implications for the government in terms of equity (property, buildings, and equipment).

The second item of the proposal addressed the record of the Board of Governors of St. Clare's Mercy Hospital. It pointed out that St. Clare's had demonstrated its excellence in quality care supported by its reputation, national recognition, and successive full accreditation since 1958. The hospital was noted for its compassion, its respect for the dignity of each person, and its working for the good of the community as a whole.

The St. Clare's board had repeatedly demonstrated willingness to rationalize services, most dramatically in the decision with respect to obstetrics, gynaecology, pediatrics, and Talbot House. These programs had special significance for the hospital and its owners, the Sisters of Mercy, but St. Clare's had agreed to transfer these programs to other health care organizations for the overall benefit of the health care system. Furthermore, St. Clare's participated fully in studies through the St. John's Hospital Council and, of all the institutions, was the most proactive in bringing the study recommendations to the St. Clare's board for consideration. The document pointed out that St. Clare's willingly assumed responsibility for the Dr. Walter Templeman Hospital on Bell Island and carried out this responsibility with no financial compensation and, up to that time (1992), without government's acceptance of that hospital's deficits.

Under the direction of the board of governors, St. Clare's became a leader in the field of health care. The hospital's pastoral care department, its management information system, its palliative care unit, Talbot House, the computerization of the patient information system, the energy conservation program, the introduction of laparoscopic cholecystectomies, a Labour Canada project involving the appropriate skill mix of nurses and nursing assistants, an employee assistance program, and an injury prevention program are examples of programs the hospital introduced to improve efficiency and effectiveness. In all these instances, the board used discretionary funds to introduce the programs. Moreover, the board successfully encouraged participation by staff members and physicians in other health boards, unions, professional organizations, and community groups.

The board of governors of St. Clare's had made great efforts to ensure representation from many different sectors of society. St. Clare's board included representatives appointed by the provincial government, the City of St. John's, Memorial University, two representatives from Bell Island, a senior representative from the labour movement, and one from each of the three Roman Catholic dioceses of Newfoundland.

The third item of the St. Clare's proposal addressed the general implications of restructuring. While the members of St. Clare's board accepted the wisdom of exploring the benefits of merging some boards, they cautioned against the creation of a large board structure encompassing many sites with a broad scope of mandates. St. Clare's had concerns that a more complex organization would see an increasing gap between patients and decision-makers as well as among staff, physicians, and senior managers. They pointed out that large organizations tend to become less personalized and more bureaucratic. St. Clare's also feared that in the government's plan, the concentration seemed to be on revising board structures rather than in issues having greater significance in improving the health care system (e.g. the distribution of physicians and evolution from institutional care to community-based care).

In its proposal, board members brought forward the concerns of the Dr. Walter Templeman Hospital on Bell Island. They pointed out the unique characteristics of Bell Island and the subsequent implications for the provision of health care for its community. In any restructuring, the representatives from Bell Island wanted to ensure that the mandate of the Dr. Walter Templeman Hospital as a community health centre would not be jeopardized if the hospital were brought under a board in St. John's that would govern several tertiary care institutions.

Before considering any options for the restructuring of boards, St. Clare's listed a number of objectives, the first being the maintenance of the same quality of care for which St. Clare's has been recognized. It was important that the new system, if implemented, would be better for patients than the present system and that there would be no weakening of St. Clare's Mercy Hospital's responsibility for knowing and responding to the health care needs of the community it served.

Other matters of importance dealt with the rights and responsibilities of the Congregation of the Sisters of Mercy, the owners of St. Clare's Mercy Hospital. In any restructuring, responsibility and accountability for the mission, values, and philosophy of St. Clare's should rest with the board of governors of St. Clare's. Furthermore, the link between the Sisters of Mercy and the board of governors should be maintained, and the Congregation of the Sisters of Mercy and the Roman Catholic Church should continue to have input into the appointment of board members. As in the past, the Sisters of Mercy should be permitted significant input into the selection and appointment of the chairperson of the board and the executive director of St. Clare's.

The proposal to Mrs. Dobbin listed the many ways in which St. Clare's had participated in planning a new model of health care and its voluntary participation in the centralization/rationalization agreement among the St. John's hospitals. St. Clare's had also demonstrated its commitment to regional planning by the difficult decisions made by the board in the sharing of services.

Finally, the document presented a number of options for any restructuring and reiterated the board's commitment to doing what was necessary to ensure the most appropriate board structure for the province's health care facilities. However, the board felt that any new structure should not result in a complex, depersonalized organization or a cumbersome structure that would lead to increased bureaucracy and added costs.[13]

In accepting the document containing the board's proposals,

---

13. Presentation of proposal by the Board of Governors of St. Clare's Mercy Hospital dealing with board restructuring, September 24, 1992, ASMSJ. All of the material dealing with this proposal has been taken directly from the original document.

Mrs. Dobbin advised the members that she would continue her discussion with other hospitals and nursing homes in the city. She anticipated that her draft report would be available in December 1992, with a final report in February 1993 before the budget speech in March.[14]

The uncertainty, and even turbulence, surrounding the government's plans for the restructuring of hospital boards, coincided with some important anniversaries. The year 1992 marked the 70th anniversary of St. Clare's as well as the 150th anniversary of the establishment of the Sisters of Mercy in Newfoundland. During the same year, 1992, the St. Clare's Mercy Hospital Auxiliary celebrated the 25th anniversary of its founding. These anniversaries provided opportunities to celebrate in various ways the mission and values of St. Clare's. Sr. Madonna Gatherall chaired the 70th anniversary committee and organized a number of events including a ceremony during which the mission statement was formally proclaimed.[15] As a lasting souvenir of this anniversary, a brochure noting the historical highlights of each decade of the hospital was prepared and distributed. On May 21, the actual anniversary of the founding of St. Clare's Mercy Hospital, a Liturgy of Thanksgiving was celebrated in the chapel. In addition to the liturgy, a number of events took place on that day, including a pictorial display and a contest for the children of hospital staff. Several times during the anniversary year, members of the hospital staff were invited to "Morning Coffee" at St. Clare's Convent (the original hospital).

Throughout this anniversary year of 1992, the mission of St. Clare's was highlighted in all the celebrations that took place. An important dimension of the mission of St. Clare's was to comply with and support the standards outlined in the health care ethics guidelines of the Canadian Conference of Catholic Bishops. Sr. Madonna Gatherall, the director of mission effectiveness, was a

14. Minutes, BOGSC, September 24, 1992, ASMSJ.
15. See appendix C.

member of both the pastoral care advisory committee and the ethics committee. In co-operation with various subcommittees, Sr. Madonna developed a number of ethical policies for St. Clare's, for instance, decisions involved in the withholding or withdrawing of artificial nutrition/hydration, cardiopulmonary resuscitation, and the withdrawal of life-sustaining treatment. These policies provided the framework for similar policies that were later developed by the ethics committee of the Health Care Corporation of St. John's.

However, during the twenty-one years since the opening of the 1972 extension to St. Clare's, the delivery of health care in Newfoundland had become more and more complex. The annual report of 1993 lists the nine major program areas that were delivered at St. Clare's. The treatment of musculoskeletal illness was carried out through programs in orthopaedic surgery and rheumatology. St. Clare's was the designated centre for care of rheumatic diseases. St. Clare's was also the centre in St. John's for elective orthopaedic surgery and single trauma. Futhermore, St. Clare's was the designated centre for thoracic surgery in St. John's, and the hospital was also named by the Department of Health as the site for any future developments in respiratory medicine.

The treatment of gastrointestinal illness was carried out through programs in gastrointestinal medicine and general surgery. In this area, also, St. Clare's was designated as the site for future developments. As a consequence of this designation, the program in general surgery at the hospital was expanded.

The provision of general internal medicine included respiratory and gastrointestinal medicine as well as cardiology and general medicine. Inpatient care, critical care, ambulatory care, emergency services, and consultation services were key components of the programs for general internal medicine.

Similarly, the provision of mental health care at St. Clare's included the same services as those available for general internal medicine with the added dimension of community outreach.

The provision of palliative care at St. Clare's included referral; assessment; inpatient care, consultation, and advice; and education and outpatient care. The philosophy accepted by the hospital recognized palliative care as a therapeutic option available to terminally ill patients and included responding to the needs of families.

In addition to these programs, the delivery of ambulatory care at St. Clare's was based on the belief that the hospital wished to provide as much health care as possible for patients without requiring them to remain overnight in hospital. Also, the emergency services offered by St. Clare's provided emergency care for patients from St. John's and the surrounding area in relation to the programs identified above. For persons who came to the emergency department in need of programs not offered by St. Clare's, the policy of the hospital was to stabilize the patient and then transfer that person to the nearest hospital where programs were available to address the patient's need.

Health education offered at St. Clare's included education for patients, students, physicians, other staff, board members, and the broader community. A key component for the provision of education was, of course, St. Clare's Mercy Hospital School of Nursing. The report pointed out that St. Clare's was a designated teaching hospital for the school of medicine at Memorial University.

The delivery of these programs required ongoing renovations of the hospital buildings. Furthermore, in 1993, computerization had been extended to include material management and the operating room management system. Through the assistance of St. Clare's Mercy Hospital Foundation, the auxiliary, the Northwest Rotary, and the Department of Health, new equipment was purchased and the energy conservation program continued. Also in 1993, the endoscopy unit became a free-standing service with an expansion to two procedure rooms.[16]

While all this activity was going on in the hospital itself, the board of governors, and particularly the chairman, Mr. Maloney, and the executive director of the hospital, Sr. Elizabeth Davis, was in constant communication with the minister of health and the deputy ministers. The minutes of a meeting of the board of governors in March 1993 record the discussion of a statement made by the minister of health to the media. In this release, the minister indicated that the government had endorsed in principle the Dobbin Report recommending a regional board structure for the province. Furthermore, the minister anticipated beginning implementation of the report over the next few months, beginning with the St. John's area.[17] In response to this, St. Clare's board wrote to Premier Clyde Wells expressing concerns over such massive reorganization of health care in the province. The letter went on to state:

If, despite these concerns, it is deemed that restructuring is appropriate and is to be implemented, we trust that your government will allow St. Clare's to maintain its mission, values and philosophy. It is our firm conviction that such protection will be in the best interests of the patients who entrust themselves to the care of this hospital. We believe that this protection can be achieved through certain conditions which will not detract from the objectives of any new regional board . . . We further request, if restructuring does take place that the health care needs of the people of Bell Island and the special status of the Dr. Walter Templeman Hospital will be protected.[18]

---

16. St. Clare's Mercy Hospital Annual Report, 1993–1994, ASMSJ.

17. Minutes, BOGSC, March 8, 1993, ASMSJ.

18 Aidan Maloney, chairperson of the Board of Governors of St. Clare's Mercy Hospital, to the Honourable Clyde K. Wells, premier of Newfoundland and Labrador, March 19, 1993, ASMSJ.

Over the next weeks and months, the pace of planning and negotiation dealing with consolidation of the boards accelerated. Several options were seriously considered and finally abandoned. On August 11, 1993, Sr. Elizabeth and Mr. Maloney were called to meet immediately with Dr. Hubert Kitchen, the minister of health. At the outset, Dr. Kitchen acknowledged that the government's planning and priorities committee had directed him to address the proposed restructuring of the hospital boards in St. John's. The minister identified three possible options for restructuring: 1) three boards, incorporating adult acute-care hospitals and children's (hospital and rehabilitation); 2) one board to govern all six facilities in St. John's; and 3) two boards (adult and children). The minister indicated that his preference was for the second option. Mr. Maloney outlined clearly the position of St. Clare's in any restructuring and the concern of the St. Clare's board for the status of Dr. Walter Templeman Hospital on Bell Island. During this meeting, the minister assured Sr. Elizabeth and Mr. Maloney that consultations with the hospital would continue.[19]

A week later, on August 20, 1993, Sr. Elizabeth and Mr. Maloney met with two other government ministers, Mr. Chuck Furey and Mr. Jim Walsh. This meeting had been requested by Mr. Maloney prior to the meeting held on August 11 with the minister of health. Both Mr. Furey and Mr. Walsh understood clearly that board restructuring would take place in St. John's and that it would involve St. Clare's. They asked for a summary of what had happened to date and for a detailed clarification of the document that St. Clare's had presented to the premier in March 1993. After discussing the contents of the St. Clare's proposal, neither minister saw any problem with the conditions and asked to be kept informed of future plans and

19. Report for the Executive Committee of the Board of Governors of St. Clare's Mercy Hospital, September 7, 1993, ASMSJ.

proposals. They were both pleased to know that Dr. Kitchen, the minister of health, was of the same opinion.[20]

On the same day, August 20, Sr. Elizabeth met with Dr. Robert Williams, the deputy minister of Health and Community Services, to outline St. Clare's position regarding restructuring. She emphasized that the Sisters of Mercy desired to remain in health care because they believe that they brought added value to the delivery of health care at St. Clare's. For his part, Dr. Williams reiterated the intention of the Department of Health to protect the status of St. Clare's as a Catholic hospital. However, Dr. Williams pointed out that the real decision-makers were the Cabinet and the premier and, in actual fact, he could not speak for any position they might take.[21] On August 26, in a meeting with Dr. Williams and Ms. Primrose Bishop, assistant deputy minister of Health and Community Services, Sr. Elizabeth repeated St. Clare's position with respect to the hospital's pre-ferred option for maintaining its own board and the non-nego-tiable principle of maintaining its status as a Catholic hospital. Dr. Williams suggested that it would be important that Sr. Marion Collins, superior general of the Sisters of Mercy, meet with Premier Clyde Wells to finalize the basic principles that involve St. Clare's in the proposed restructuring. One of these issues might be that under any new structure imposed by government, the buildings comprising St. Clare's Mercy Hospital would be leased to the government. However, Sr. Elizabeth repeated her concern that, although this discussion revolved around details of amended incorporation and a lease, no decision had been made by the Sisters of Mercy or by St. Clare's board for voluntary par-ticipation in any proposed restructuring.[22]

In order to clarify the status of St. Clare's as a Catholic

---

20. Ibid.

21. Sr. Elizabeth Davis, "Activities re Proposed Restructuring of Hospital Boards," Report for the Executive Committee of the Board of Governors of St. Clare's Mercy Hospital, September 7, 1993, ASMSJ.

22. Ibid.

hospital under the government's plan for restructuring, on August 30, Sr. Elizabeth consulted Father Everett MacNeil of the Catholic Health Association of Canada (CHAC). Father MacNeil pointed out that a hospital can only be called Catholic if the archbishop so designates it. Therefore, St. Clare's would have to have the approval of the archbishop of St. John's for any agreement that would be made with the provincial government. On the same day, Sr. Marion Collins and Sr. Elizabeth held a telephone consultation with Father Frank Morrissey, the leading canon lawyer in Canada. Father Morrissey reiterated the points that Father MacNeil had made but felt that it might be necessary to inform the Vatican in Rome about the restructuring after it happened to let them know what the protections would be with respect to the Health Care Ethics Guide. However, Father Morrissey saw the necessity for restructuring and the need for Catholic institutions to participate positively in that restructuring.[23]

On November 24, 1993, the minister of health, Dr. Hubert Kitchen, announced in the House of Assembly that the government had made the decision to have all the hospitals in the St. John's region governed by one board. This board was to be responsible for the General Hospital; St. Clare's Mercy Hospital and the Dr. Walter Templeman Hospital, Bell Island; the Grace General Hospital; the Waterford Hospital; the Dr. Charles A. Janeway Child Health Centre; and the Children's Rehabilitation Centre.[24] The minister concluded his statement as follows:

> In the very near future I will be appointing the new board. In doing so, I shall be having further consultation with existing

---

23. Ibid.

24. Newfoundland and Labrador, First Session of the Forty-Second General Assembly of Newfoundland, *House of Assembly Proceedings* 42, no. 21 (November 24, 1993), preliminary report, Hansard, 713, ASMSJ.

boards in the St. John's area for nominations to the new board. I would anticipate that the new board will assume its official responsibility for facilities in the St. John's region by April 1 [1995], if possible, certainly early in the next fiscal year. This will allow a transition period, during which the new board will work with existing boards in the St. John's region.[25]

Early in 1994, the Health Care Corporation of St. John's was established to integrate hospital services in the St. John's region. The St. Clare's Mercy Hospital Annual Report in 1994 referred to the formation of this regional health board and included the following statement:

To ensure that the mission, philosophy and values of St. Clare's as a Catholic hospital will be maintained and protected within the new board structure, the Congregation's Superior General [of the Congregation of the Sisters of Mercy], the Sisters of Mercy and the present Board of Governors of St. Clare's have worked with the Premier and officials from various provincial government departments. The discussions have been positive and the St. Clare's community is confident that a proposed agreement will be approved by government. Contingent on the approval of the agreement, the Sisters of Mercy have named Sister Charlotte Fitzpatrick and Ms. Eleanor Bonnell as our representatives to the Board.[26]

In the midst of all the uncertainty surrounding the delivery of health care, St. Clare's continued its tradition of reaching out to suffering people in the community. On January 25, 1994, a state-of-the-art sleep studies laboratory was officially opened. The only one of its type in the province, the St. Clare's Mercy Hospital Sleep Studies Program helped diagnose hundreds of

---

25. Ibid.
26. St. Clare's Mercy Hospital Annual Report, 1993–1994, ASMSJ.

people suffering from sleep disorders. Furthermore, it demonstrated the commitment of St. Clare's Mercy Hospital to being a leader in health care delivery.[27]

In the same month, January 1994, renovations were completed to the ambulatory clinics in orthopaedics and surgery. A dedicated satellite diagnostic imaging unit provided for a more rapid diagnosis of a patient's illness and quicker treatment. These renovations were the first phase of a broader plan that saw improved space for the emergency department, medical clinics and psychiatry. The renovation to ambulatory clinics in the most patient accessible area of the hospital reflected the hospital's determination to address emerging trends in the health care system. In addition, St. Clare's enhanced the area of critical care by creating a medical/surgical stepdown unit of six beds.[28]

But while ministry at the hospital was being carried on as usual, with most patients unaware of the big changes that were soon to take place, the chair of the board of governors, Aidan Maloney, and the executive director of the hospital, Sr. Elizabeth Davis, were having frequent discussions with various levels of government and with the leadership of the Sisters of Mercy on the plan for restructuring the health care boards. On August 19, 1994, the Board of Governors of St. Clare's Mercy Hospital held a special emergency meeting. The first item on the agenda for this special meeting was the presentation of the final draft agreement between the Congregation of the Sisters of Mercy, St. Clare's Mercy Hospital, and the provincial government. Members of the board were informed that the minister of health and the deputy minister had accepted the document and the minister had agreed to bring it to Cabinet for final approval. The superior general and the council of the Sisters of Mercy and the archbishop of St. John's had approved the draft agreement. At this meeting, the document

---

27. Ibid.
28. Ibid.

was presented to the Board of Governors of St. Clare's Mercy Hospital for its approval. Sr. Elizabeth Davis reviewed the contents of the agreement and highlighted areas where changes had been made to the previous draft. The most significant change related to the transfer of ownership of the land and buildings from the Congregation of the Sisters of Mercy to the provincial government with a twenty-year schedule of payments. Members of the board discussed the guarantees in the agreement to ensure that the mission, philosophy, and ethics of St. Clare's would be maintained in the spirit and tradition of the Sisters of Mercy. Loss of ownership of the land and buildings was discussed in detail. It was agreed that the continuation of the mission could be separated from the right of ownership. The continuing liability for the Sisters of Mercy in owning the property when they could no longer direct the governance of the facility was noted as a serious concern. Members of the board decided that there were sufficient guarantees to ensure the continuation of the hospital's ministry and that the transfer of title to the property for an acceptable sum of money would be a wise decision. The board of governors voted to accept the agreement.[29]

At this same meeting, on August 19, 1994, a letter of resignation was received from Sr. Elizabeth Davis who, a month earlier, had been appointed the first chief executive officer of the new Health Care Corporation of St. John's. Sr. Elizabeth was to begin her new duties on October 3, 1994. Also at this meeting, Sr. Marion Collins, superior general of the Sisters of Mercy, presented a letter nominating Dr. Sean Conroy as acting executive director of St. Clare's and the Dr. Walter Templeman Hospital effective September 1, 1994. Dr. Conroy's appointment was an interim one in light of the uncertainty about the management structure under the new board of the Health Care Corporation of St. John's.

---

29. Minutes, BOGSC, August 19, 1994, ASMSJ.

Before Sr. Elizabeth left St. Clare's to take up her new position with the Health Care Corporation, Sr. Madonna Gatherall of the mission effectiveness department planned a farewell celebration. The event began with a welcome by Dr. Sean Conroy and a "Celebration of Gift" led by Sr. Phyllis Corbett. After this, a number of departments and services within the hospital expressed gratitude to Sr. Elizabeth for her dedication and commitment to St. Clare's, especially during the difficult period of restructuring.

Of course, everything that happens at St. Clare's is related to the mission of the hospital—the transfer of obstetrics (1992), the opening of LeMarchant House (1994), the opening of ambulatory clinics, the opening of the intermediate care unit, the opening of the renovated emergency department and medical/surgical clinics (1994), and the official opening and dedication of the newly renovated endoscopy suite in memory of Dr. Garrett Brownrigg (1995). Dr. Garrett M. Brownrigg had been both chief of surgery and chief of staff at St. Clare's from 1958 to 1977. Throughout his career, Dr. Brownrigg was dedicated to the spirit and mission of St. Clare's. He was deeply involved in the negotiations with Memorial University that saw St. Clare's recognized as a teaching hospital. In 1948, Dr. Brownrigg was made a Commander of the Order of the British Empire. In 1968, he received the honourary degree of doctor of science from Memorial University in acknowledgement of his contributions in the field of medicine. It was appropriate that Dr. Brownrigg's memory would be perpetuated at St. Clare's by the dedication of a special medical unit in his name. This event, as well as all the other significant initiatives undertaken by St. Clare's, was marked by celebrations planned by Sr. Madonna Gatherall and her mission effectiveness team.

However, at St. Clare's things never stand still. Further changes were about to take place. In order to allow the provincial government to proceed with its restructuring program, the Sisters of Mercy agreed to transfer St. Clare's Mercy Hospital to the government. On December 8, 1994, the Congregation of the Sisters of Mercy signed the agreement to sell the hospital buildings to the government and transfer the operation of the hospital to the Board of Directors of the Health Care Corporation of St. John's.[30] Under the agreement, the mission, values, philosophy, and ethical principles of St. Clare's would be continued and the ministry of the Sisters of Mercy and their presence in the hospital would continue. Furthermore, the agreement gave the Sisters of Mercy the right to nominate two persons to the board of directors of the Health Care Corporation.[31] In addition, the Sisters of Mercy retained the right to approve the person who has direct management responsibility for the St. Clare's Mercy Hospital site. As well, the Sisters of Mercy have the right to remain at St. Clare's Convent under the same conditions as obtained at the time the agreement came into effect, April 1, 1995. This coincided with the change of governance from the Board of Governors of St. Clare's Mercy Hospital to the Board of Directors of the Health Care Corporation of St. John's.[32]

The Sisters of Mercy recognize that, with the many technical and financial changes in health care, there had to be changes in the organization of tertiary care for the province. However, they also felt that they wished to remain part of the ministry of healing at St. Clare's Mercy Hospital. Therefore, the agreement the Sisters of Mercy signed with the

---

30. The ministerial statement announcing the agreement between the Government of Newfoundland and Labrador and the Sisters of Mercy is found in appendix E.

31. The first two persons appointed under this agreement were Sr. Charlotte Fitzpatrick and Ms. Eleanor Bonnell.

32. "Agreement between the Sisters of Mercy and the Government of Newfoundland and Labrador," *Promptly Speaking* 2, no. 12 (December 8, 1994), 1. RG 10/9/221, ASMSJ.

Government of Newfoundland and Labrador allowed the structural changes to happen while at the same time ensuring that the sisters continued to influence health care delivery not only at St. Clare's Mercy Hospital but within the Health Care Corporation of St. John's and within the province.

During the February 1995 meeting of the board, Dr. Conroy advised that Sr. Elizabeth, on behalf of Mrs. Eileen Young, chairperson of the board of the Health Care Corporation of St. John's, had written the chairs of the various foundations with respect to preparing a bylaw statement which allows the foundation boards at the various institutions to remain in place when the institution boards cease to exist. Sr. Elizabeth suggested the following draft statement for St. Clare's Mercy Hospital:

> The purpose of St. Clare's Mercy Hospital Foundation shall be to support and enhance the work and the goals of St. Clare's, in accordance with the Foundation's Articles, Continuance and By-laws [sic]. In the Articles of Continuance and By-laws [sic], the St. Clare's Mercy Hospital Board of Governors shall be replaced by the Board of Trustees of the Health Care Corporation of St. John's.[33]

March 25, 1995, had been set aside as the date for the transfer of governance of the regional health care facilities, including St. Clare's Mercy Hospital, to the Health Care Corporation of St. John's. Three days prior to this, on March 22, 1995, a ceremony took place at St. Clare's to mark the transfer of governance. The theme for the ceremony was "Remembering the Past, Celebrating the Present, Shaping the Future." Through music, symbol, and word, five areas were presented for reflection—mission, history/culture/tradition/,

---

33. Minutes, BOGSC, February 23, 1995, ASMSJ.

community, material resources, and programs and services of the hospital—all of which were seen as gifts that were passed on to the newly formed Health Care Corporation of St. John's. The ceremony concluded with a blessing by the archbishop of St. John's, Most Reverend James MacDonald. Dr. Sean Conroy, acting executive director of St. Clare's Mercy Hospital, presented the archbishop; Sr. Marion Collins, superior general of the Congregation of the Sisters of Mercy; and Mr. Aidan Maloney, chair of the board of governors, with a framed photograph of the stained glass window in St. Clare's oratory in recognition of their committed and dedicated service to the hospital. Many members of the staff of St. Clare's were present for the ceremony and all were invited to remain for refreshments. That evening, members of the board of governors and their spouses were invited to a special dinner sponsored by the Congregation of the Sisters of Mercy. This event provided the sisters with an opportunity to express the appreciation of their congregation to the members of the board for their leadership and dedicated service to St. Clare's Mercy Hospital.

On March 25, 1995, in a press release, Sr. Elizabeth Davis, president and chief executive officer of the Health Care Corporation of St. John's, announced the transfer of governance of the eight health care facilities in St. John's from local boards to the Health Care Corporation. The release read as follows:

At a ceremony today, eight Health Care facilities in the St. John's region transferred their governance to the Health Care Corporation of St. John's. The Board of Trustees of the Children's Rehabilitation Centre, the General Hospital, the Janeway Child Heath Care Centre, the Salvation Army Grace General Hospital, St. Clare's Mercy Hospital and the Waterford Hospital were consolidated into one regional board in an effort to facilitate effective patient care delivery and efficiency of resource utilization. Also affected in the transfer process were the Leonard A. Miller Centre, formerly under the Board of Trustees of the General Hospital Corporation and the Dr. Walter Templeman Hospital on Bell Island, formerly under the Board of Governors of St. Clare's Mercy Hospital . . . The Chairperson of the Board of Trustees for each facility took their turn in formally signing over governance to the Health Care Corporation of St. John's at the ceremony.[34]

---

34. Sr. Elizabeth Davis, president and chief executive officer of the Health Care Corporation of St. John's, March 25, 1995, ASMSJ. At this ceremony, Mr. Aidan Maloney, chairperson of the Board of Governors of St. Clare's Mercy Hospital, signed on behalf of St. Clare's.

THE LIGHTS THAT WE HAVE KINDLED

We thank Thee for the lights that we have kindled . . .
—T. S. Eliot

On March 30, 1995, Mr. Aidan Maloney chaired the final meeting of the Board of Governors of St. Clare's Mercy Hospital. The role of Mr. Maloney in the growth and development of St. Clare's cannot be overstated. With knowledge informed by keen insight and a deep appreciation of the mission, philosophy, and ethical principals of St. Clare's, he had guided the board of governors, the hospital, and the Congregation of the Sisters of Mercy through the turbulent days of restructuring. With tireless interest and dedication, he attended countless meetings with various levels of government and with other health care organizations. Throughout years of negotiations, Mr. Maloney steadfastly upheld the principles, the values, and the philosophy of St. Clare's Mercy Hospital. He was unwavering in his conviction that these values, philosophy, and ethical principles, so integral to St. Clare's, were essential ingredients of every modern-day health care system. Mr. Maloney's convictions were among the factors that lead to an agreement acceptable to the provincial government, the Congregation of the Sisters of Mercy, the St. Clare's board of governors, and the physicians and staff of the hospital.

Two years before the sale of St. Clare's to the provincial government, Mr. Maloney's efforts on behalf of St. Clare's and the health care system were acknowledged when he received an honourary doctor of laws degree from Memorial University

181

of Newfoundland and the Order of Canada from the governor general.

At the final meeting of the board of governors on March 30, 1995, Dr. Sean Conroy, acting executive director, expressed gratitude to the board and, on behalf of the hospital, presented to each member a framed collage relating to the life of the hospital. On the following day, March 31, a complimentary dinner was served to all staff, physicians, and volunteers at St. Clare's as part of the celebrations marking the transfer of governance.

The sale of St. Clare's Mercy Hospital and its transfer to new governance marked a significant milestone in the life of the hospital. Nevertheless, its mission, values, ethics, and philosophy remained the same—to care for the sick and dying with competence and compassion, carried out in the spirit and tradition of the Sisters of Mercy. The mission affirms the dignity and uniqueness of each person, fosters holistic healing and promotes the pastoral care of all patients.

As a result of agreements made between the provincial government and the private owners of health care facilities in the St. John's region, the Health Care Corporation of St. John's established advisory councils that operated within the various health care institutions. One such council was the St. Clare's Mercy Hospital Advisory Council that was established in 1995. According to the terms of reference, the St. Clare's advisory council advises the board of the Health Care Corporation so that the board may ensure that the mission, values, and philosophy of St. Clare's reflect the spirit and tradition of the Sisters of Mercy and provide initiatives to promote these principles and, further, ensure that St. Clare's operates within the health care ethics guidelines outlined in the statement of principles appended to the agreement with the government.

The members of the St. Clare's advisory council are appointed by the board of the Health Care Corporation on the nomination of the congregational leader of the Sisters of Mercy. The council is composed of eight appointed members, two of whom are representatives of the Congregation of the Sisters of Mercy. The congregational leader of the Sisters of Mercy is an ex officio member of the advisory council as are the representatives of the mission effectiveness committee, ethics committee, and pastoral care department.

In the day-to-day activities of St. Clare's, the on-site manager of pastoral care is appointed by the chief executive officer of the Health Care Corporation of St. John's with the approval of the Congregation of the Sisters of Mercy. At the time when the ownership and governance of St. Clare's Mercy Hospital was assumed by the Government of Newfoundland and Labrador, Sr. Diane Smyth continued as divisional manager of pastoral care and ethics at St. Clare's. The director of mission effectiveness is appointed by the Congregation of the Sisters of Mercy and reports to the on-site executive management representative at St. Clare's. At the time of writing, Sr. Madonna Gatherall is the director of mission effectiveness at St. Clare's.

The change in the ownership and governance of St. Clare's required a rethinking of the mission statement of the hospital. The 1991 mission statement had articulated the Christian values on which St. Clare's was originally founded. The key element of this statement was that St. Clare's is dedicated to the healing ministry of Jesus and the Church, through being faithful to the mission and values of Jesus, and to witness to his spirit, particularly his mercy and compassion.[1] The agreement signed between the Government of Newfoundland and Labrador and the Sisters of Mercy to transfer ownership of the hospital to the province included a revision of the mission statement to reflect the new realities.[2]

---

1. See appendix C.
2. See appendix C.

In May 1995, Sr. Phyllis Corbett was appointed administrator of St. Clare's, a position she held for a year. Sr. Phyllis was the last Sister of Mercy to hold this post at St. Clare's Mercy Hospital.

Although St. Clare's is operated under the jurisdiction of the Health Care Corporation of St. John's, the Sisters of Mercy continue to minister to the sick in the hospital. Sr. Diane Smyth is the divisional manager of the pastoral care department. At the time of writing, in addition to her duties at St. Clare's and the Miller Centre, Sr. Diane is also temporarily the associate director of pastoral care of Eastern Health, the regional health authority that has provided health care services in eastern Newfoundland since 2005. In this capacity she will give leadership to the pastoral care services of the pastoral care and ethics department of Eastern Health. The religious/spiritual care of patients, staff, and family is coordinated through this department.

When the hospital was smaller and a large number of Sisters of Mercy ministered to patients, St. Clare's had a distinctive religious ambience. For many years, St. Clare's had a resident chaplain, a Roman Catholic priest, up to the time of Monsignor James Fennessey's retirement in 1990, and clergy from many religious denominations were frequent visitors. However, along with all the other changes that have taken place at the hospital, there is no longer a resident chaplain. Roman Catholic, Anglican, United, Salvation Army, and Pentecostal churches have appointed chaplains to minister at St. Clare's. A number of pastoral volunteers from all denominations provide spiritual and religious care to patients at St. Clare's. Sr. Diane Smyth described the function of the pastoral care department at St. Clare's as follows:

> Pastoral Care at St. Clare's is like the soul of St. Clare's, that spiritual dimension that gives it life, the bonding agent that ensures a connectedness in the many complex and technical aspects of a modern hospital. Pastoral Care is the spirit of St.

Clare's that is a manifestation of God's Spirit and God's presence.[3]

In addition to the pastoral care department, there is at St. Clare's another group of dedicated volunteers who comprise the St. Clare's Mercy Hospital Auxiliary. Since its establishment in 1967, the St. Clare's Mercy Hospital Auxiliary has worked quietly—behind the scenes for the most part—to promote the ministry of the hospital. In an address given on the occasion of the fortieth anniversary of the establishment of the St. Clare's Mercy Hospital Auxiliary, Sr. Madonna Gatherall, the director of mission effectiveness, made the following comments:

> Little did Sr. M. Fabian [Hennebury] realize what a fabulous initiative it was when she invited a small group of friends of St. Clare's to a meeting in January 1967. The records state that at that meeting the first Auxiliary was formed with Joan Parker as the first president and Sister Mary Aidan [Howell] as the first director.[4]

Sr. Madonna continued her address by listing some of the contributions provided to St. Clare's by the auxiliary during the forty years since its establishment—several kinds of monitors for coronary care, including ECG and pulse defibrillators; EEG; respirators; stretcher frames; gas sterilizer; patient stretchers; an ultrasound machine and equipment; nuclear medicine machinery; wheelchairs; geriatric chairs; intensive care beds; labour beds; delivery beds; and donations throughout the whole range of services of the hospital with some items

---

3. Sr. Diane Smyth, unpublished manuscript, RG 10/89/168, ASMSJ.

4. Sr. Madonna Gatherall, Address given on the occasion of the fortieth anniversary of St. Clare's Mercy Hospital Auxiliary, St. John's, October 10, 2007, ASMSJ.

costing over fifty thousand dollars. At the time of the establishment of the St. Clare's Mercy Hospital Foundation, the auxiliary pledged $250,000 to the foundation to help it get started, so that up to the end of the year 2006, donations to the hospital totalled close to two million dollars.

Perhaps the best known of the auxiliary's activities are the early bird sale, the card parties, the ticket sales, the charity ball, the craft workshops, and the gift shop. The gift shop is a service provided by the auxiliary that responds to the needs of patients, staff, and visitors. In addition to monetary donations, there are various services of a non-monetary nature that the auxiliary provides at St. Clare's. Among these are the provision of a library cart for all patients on the floors and assistance to the Red Cross clinics, the Cancer Society, the Kidney Foundation, hairdressing services, the nursing school library, and other services as required. Direct assistance is offered to patients through feeding and friendly visiting programs, whether through writing letters, making phone calls, translation, or just by being present. Included in these latter services is the work of the candystripers (now known as volunteens).[5]

In her address, Sr. Madonna pointed out that because times have changed since the establishment of the auxiliary in 1967, different needs are presented today and the services offered by the auxiliary have changed to correspond to these needs. Nevertheless, there are some things that never change and among these is the presence of members of the St. Clare's Mercy Hospital Auxiliary throughout the hospital every day. Their presence keeps alive the mission and values of St. Clare's—values of care, compassion, service, hospitality, respect, kindness, and presence—those values of the heart, making the motto of St. Clare's, "Mercy Above All," alive and active within the hospital. St. Clare's benefited a great deal from the presence and services of the members of the auxiliary

5 Ibid.

over the years and for this St. Clare's will always be grateful. In her final remarks, Sr. Madonna acknowledged the contribution of Sharon Dawe. For twenty-four years, Ms. Dawe had been responsible for the organization, administration, and coordination of volunteer services at St. Clare's.[6]

Meanwhile, by the end of the year 1999, the government's plans for the restructuring of the health care boards had been accomplished under the direction of the president and chief executive officer of the St. John's Health Care Corporation, Sr. Elizabeth Davis. This complex and difficult assignment had taken six years to bring to fruition. On March 14, 2000, Sr. Elizabeth announced her resignation as chief executive officer. In a letter to the staff members, physicians, and volunteers, Sr. Elizabeth wrote:

> Most of you are aware that I had signed a five-year contract with the Board in October 1994. I have remained an extra year to finish the work the Board asked me to do in 1994—to provide leadership to enable all of us together to achieve three goals (1) to bring our new organization together in administrative and support areas; (2) to integrate our direct care clinical services; and (3) to complete our site redevelopment project. With the transfer of services from the Salvation Army Grace General Hospital and Janeway Child Health Centre during this summer, I will have fulfilled the mandate the Board gave me. Together we have redesigned and developed a new administrative, clinical and physical infrastructure.[7]

For its part, the Government of Newfoundland and Labrador, in a news release dated March 14, 2000, expressed

---

6. Ibid

7. Sr. Elizabeth Davis to staff members, physicians, and volunteers, March 14, 2000, ASMSJ.

appreciation to Sr. Elizabeth for her wise guidance during the difficult period of restructuring:

As the board's first CEO, Sister Elizabeth assumed many responsibilities including: the consolidation of the Health Care Corporation, the integration of administrative and support functions, the integration of clinical services, and the implementation of site redevelopment. Sister Elizabeth has also been responsible for overseeing the construction of the new Janeway Children's Health and Rehabilitation Centre adjacent to the existing Health Sciences Center in St. John's. With the new Janeway scheduled to open later this year, Sister Elizabeth will have been successful in completing the mandate of her position as she identified it six years ago.

"It will be difficult to find someone to fill Sister Elizabeth's shoes," said Minister [Roger] Grimes. "In leading the province's largest health board, she has been both committed and dedicated. She brought a clear perspective and understanding of the intricacies of what this position required. I would like to thank her personally for the outstanding work she has done and I especially want to commend her on the success she has had in leading the St. John's hospitals through a significant redevelopment phase."[8]

During her tenure as chief executive officer of the Health Care Corporation, Sr. Elizabeth was faced with many difficult decisions. One of her hardest tasks was the actual restructuring of the St. John's health care system, in the course of which management positions were reduced by forty percent. Nevertheless, in spite of harsh criticism, Sr. Elizabeth was convinced that these decisions were the right ones, and she moved ahead. Toward the end of her mandate

---

8. Newfoundland and Labrador, Health and Community Services, news release, March 14, 2000, RG 10/14/68, ASMSJ.

as chief executive officer, she remarked, "While I never doubted the direction was the right move for us in the future, the price we had to pay to go in that direction was very difficult . . . You can't have it both ways. You can't be saying you want to make this world better, but then not be ready to work at the hard thing required to make it better."[9]

When announcing her resignation from the St. John's Health Care Corporation, Sr. Elizabeth indicated that she wanted to return to the field of study and teaching the Hebrew and Christian Scriptures, a field she left when the Congregation of the Sisters of Mercy asked her to assume health care administration. And so, after a short rest, Sr. Elizabeth returned to the University of Toronto to continue her studies. However, her peaceful existence with her books was interrupted a year later, in 2002, when the Government of Newfoundland and Labrador asked her to act as one of three members of a Royal Commission to study the province's place in Canada. This was a year-long task and involved a great deal of travel to many communities in Newfoundland and Labrador as well as the work of summarizing the hundreds of briefs that had been presented to the commission and writing the final report. When this work had been completed, Sr. Elizabeth returned to her books and her studies. Nevertheless, because of her wide experience in so many areas, she is in constant demand as a speaker at conferences and conventions, not only in Canada, but also in other parts of the world. She has been the recipient of many awards from universities and health and business organizations. The latest honour received by Sr. Elizabeth was the honourary degree of doctor of laws from the University of Manitoba on May 15, 2009. The citation was delivered by Dr. Arnold Naimark, who remarked:

Sister Davis' outstanding contributions and the depth of her

---

9. Steve Bartlett, "Sister of Mercy," *The Express*, March 17, 2000, 5.

influence on leaders in health care is evidenced by the many honours and awards bestowed on her, including: Honorary Fellowship Royal College of Physicians and Surgeons of Canada, Alumna of the Year Memorial University of Newfoundland, Member Order of Canada, Doctor of Laws (*honoris causa*) Memorial University, Award for Excellence in Health Care Administration Canadian Healthcare [*sic*] Association, Performance Citation Award Catholic Health Association of Canada, Humanitarian of the Year Award Canadian Red Cross Newfoundland and Labrador Chapter, Woman of Distinction Award YM/YWCA St. John's Newfoundland, and Citizen of the Year, Knights of Columbus of Newfoundland and Labrador.[10]

In June 2009, Sr. Elizabeth Davis was elected congregational leader of the Sisters of Mercy of Newfoundland. For the next four years at least, Sr. Elizabeth's task will be to lead her congregation in exploring new frontiers and facing new challenges and daring new initiatives so that God's love and mercy may continue to inform and direct the lives and ministries of the Sisters of Mercy of Newfoundland

Interwoven with the founding, the growth, and the development of St. Clare's is the story of the Sisters of Mercy in Newfoundland. More than one hundred Sisters of Mercy have worked at St. Clare's in a variety of ministries—nursing, administration, pastoral care, environmental services, office management, pharmacy, medical records, laboratory, X-ray, dietary, mission, and education. The contribution of each one has been essential to the growth and development of St. Clare's and to the ministry of the Sisters of Mercy. There is no record of the thousands of ways in which the sisters and their colleagues at the hospital brought renewed hope and comfort to suffering people.

---

10. Dr. Arnold Naimark, Citation delivered at University of Manitoba Convocation, Winnipeg, May 15, 2009.

As a reminder of and a tribute to the sisters who ministered at St. Clare's Mercy Hospital, the Congregation of the Sisters of Mercy commissioned local artist Gerald Squires and his daughter, Esther, to design and execute a mural to be placed in the front lobby of the hospital. Planning for the mural began in the year 2002, when Sr. Madonna Gatherall, Sr. Diane Smyth, and Sr. Monica Hickey invited members of the hospital staff to share ideas regarding a suitable and fitting way to acknowledge the story of St. Clare's. The consensus was to portray various moments in the life of St. Clare's over the decades in raku ceramic. Gerald Squires prepared sketches of six panels that were refined over the next eight months. They included sketches of three Sisters of Mercy, to represent the founding sisters, and Dr. John Murphy and Archbishop E. P. Roche, as well as the original St. Clare's building, the "White House." Woven through the other panels are sketches of the buildings that were added—the school of nursing, the chapel wing, and the 1939, 1962, and 1972 buildings. Images of the various services provided by the hospital were also included. It was agreed that the sixth panel would be one that would carry the theme of the other five and the text agreed upon was "God's mercy is from generation to generation."[11] Underneath the panels, the motto of St. Clare's, "Mercy Above All," is inscribed in English and Latin, between which, the word "Mercy" is written in the languages of the province of Newfoundland and Labrador: English, French, Innu-aimun, Inuktitut, and Mi'kmaq. The mural was executed in raku, a Japanese technique of an unusual ceramic firing that uses fire, smoke, water, and air to complete the double-firing process.

On December 4, 2004, the mural panels were affixed to sheets of black granite and placed on the wall opposite the main elevators in the main lobby of the hospital in preparation for the dedication and unveiling. This part of the work was carried out by Newfoundland Granite Ltd.

---

11. Luke 1:50 (New Revised Standard Version).

The ritual of the dedication of the mural took place on December 6, 2004, and began with greetings from Mr. George Tilley, chief executive officer of the Health Care Corporation of St. John's. Three members of the advisory council of St. Clare's, Sr. Madonna Gatherall, Ina MacLean, and Brendan Rumsey, explained the context for the mural—yesterday, today, and tomorrow. Sr. Diane Smyth led the prayer of dedication that included thanksgiving to God for the many blessings bestowed on St. Clare's over the years and a prayer for God's continued blessing on all who continue to build on this legacy of mercy and compassion. Following the prayer, the mural was unveiled by Sr. Helen Harding, congregational leader of the Sisters of Mercy, and John Abbott, chair of the Health Care Corporation of St. John's. The creator of the mural, Mr. Gerald Squires, spoke on behalf of himself and his daughter, Esther. He noted that the inspiration for the title of his sculpture, "For mercy has a human heart," is taken from the poem, "Divine Image," from *Songs of Innocence* by William Blake.

While the dedication of the mural was an acknowledgement of the many years of dedicated service of the Sisters of Mercy to the sick and dying, the sisters who attended the ceremony left with a feeling of nostalgia and a certain degree of sadness. There is no doubt that, for the Sisters of Mercy, the past thirty years marked a period of diminishment—declining numbers of sisters, the rising average age of the congregation, ministries relinquished, and buildings sold. All of this had an effect on the ministry of the sisters at St. Clare's. It may be difficult for some to appreciate the real suffering involved in these losses. Each and every Sister of Mercy has made real and personal sacrifices to initiate and support the ministries of the congregation for the sake of the mission, which is to further the reign of God among all peoples and nations. It is painful to realize that some ministries that were so much part of our lives as women religious have disappeared forever.

But this is not the whole story any more than the phenomenal growth of the congregation in the 1950s and 1960s reflected the life and values of the Sisters of Mercy. At this time in our history, the Sisters of Mercy are engaged in a variety of ministries: in direct care of the sick and the aged at St. Patrick's Mercy Home; in pastoral care at St. Clare's and other health care institutions; in working with persons living with HIV and AIDS; in outreach to the poor at the Gathering Place in St. John's; in food banks all over the province; in visitation to the poor and the sick in every place where the sisters live; in parish outreach programs; in sacramental programs at the parish level; and in parish administration in places where there is no resident priest.

Nevertheless, we—the Sisters of Mercy—are asking ourselves hard questions. What have we learned from all the successes and the failures that have been part of our lives? How does all this relate to our part in the Paschal Mystery of dying and rising with Christ? Have we experienced God in the diminishment that has marked us for the last number of years? Are we willing to move into new frontiers in our search for the Living God and to be messengers of God's love to all those we meet? And what has all of this to do with St. Clare's Mercy Hospital?

The agreement between the Sisters of Mercy and the Government of Newfoundland and Labrador sees the continuation of the mission, values, philosophy, and ethical principles of St. Clare's. Furthermore, it ensures that the ministry of the Sisters of Mercy and their presence in the hospital are maintained.[12] Up to the present time, the presence and the charism of the Sisters of Mercy are still very much part of the life of St. Clare's because of the ministry of the sisters in pastoral care, mission effectiveness, and through our involvement in promoting the mission of the hospital as articulated in the mission statement.

---

12. "Agreement between the Sisters of Mercy and the Government of Newfoundland and Labrador," *Promptly Speaking* 2, no. 12 (December 8, 1994), 1. RG 10/9/221, ASMSJ.

Sr. M. Fabian Hennebury summed up the story of St. Clare's when she wrote:

> Someone has said that the pioneers of any great venture spin the golden threads which weave an undying tradition. The tradition that the . . . Sisters of St. Clare's have left the Hospital is one of dedication, mercy, kindness and hard work. To them and to all who have assisted them may be applied the words of the Lord Himself, "I was poor and hungry, sick and lonely and you cared for Me."[13]

Hopefully, even a quick glance through the contents of this book will justify the title, "The Mustard Seed," for the story of St. Clare's Mercy Hospital can, in truth, be likened to the parable of the mustard seed.[14] From very small, uncertain beginnings, it has grown into a large, modern hospital.

Although no longer owned and administered by the Sisters of Mercy, it continues to bear the name St. Clare's Mercy Hospital as a perpetual reminder of the sacrifice and dedication of a group of women who devoted their lives in service to sick and suffering humanity. These women were assisted in their efforts by dedicated and hard-working members of the board of governors of St. Clare's; by doctors, nurses, and medical technicians; and by pastoral care workers and other staff who toiled day in and day out to maintain the high standards of care that have been, and remain today, a mark of St. Clare's. Throughout its history, St. Clare's has been supported by the Roman Catholic Church in Newfoundland, and particularly by successive archbishops of the Archdiocese of St. John's, and by the many friends of St. Clare's who have contributed, in various ways, to providing the latest in medical equipment so that St. Clare's can meet the high standards required of hospitals today.

---

13. Hennebury, "St. Clare's," ASMSJ, 56.
14. Matthew 13:31–32 (New Revised Standard Version).

As we look back over the eighty-eight years since 1922, the Sisters of Mercy of Newfoundland feel a sense of joy and thanksgiving for what has been accomplished in and through St. Clare's Mercy Hospital. Our prayer is that the motto of the hospital, "Mercy Above All," will continue to be the distinguishing feature of St. Clare's Mercy Hospital in the years that lie ahead.

> *We thank Thee for the lights that we*
> *have kindled . . .*
> *We thank Thee who hast moved us to building,*
> *to finding, to forming . . .*
> T. S. Eliot[15]

---

15. T. S. Eliot, "Choruses from 'The Rock' X," in *A Guide to the Selected Poems of T. S. Eliot*, 6th ed., by B. C. Southam (New York: Barnes and Noble, 1970) 256.

Appendix A

St. Clare's Mercy Hospital

Sisters Who Ministered at St. Clare's Mercy Hospital

Sr. M. Magdalen Baker, RN
Sr. M. Perpetua Bown
Sr. M. Joseph Byrne, RN
Sr. M. Antonia Carroll, RN
Sr. M. Eugenio Carroll
Sr. Helen Caule
Sr. M. Placide Conway
Sr. Phyllis Corbett, RN
Sr. M. Lucina Cowley
Sr. M. Noel Croke
Sr. Elizabeth Davis
Sr. M. Leo Davis, RN
Sr. Patricia Marie Decker
Sr. M. Teresita Dobbin
Sr. M. Agnes Doyle
Sr. Rosalie Dwyer, RN
Sr. M. Benedicta Fitzgibbon
Sr. Charlotte Fitzpatrick
Sr. M. Gabriel Fleming
Sr. Eileen Flynn
Sr. M. Dominica Flynn
Sr. M. Scholastica Flynn
Sr. Patricia Gallant
Sr. Madonna Gatherall

197

Sr. M. Michael Gillis
Sr. M. Bernard Gladney, RN
Sr. M. Ita Glynn
Sr. M. Catherine Greene
Sr. M. Kieran Hartery, RN
Sr. M. Carmelita Hartigan
Sr. M. Carmelita Hartman (USA)
Sr. M. Fabian Hennebury, RN
Sr. M. Mark Hennebury, RN
Sr. Monica Hickey
Sr. M. Patricia Hogan
Sr. M. Aidan Howell, RN
Sr. M. Zita Hyde
Sr. Rosaline Hynes, NA
Sr. Jean Jenkinson, RN
Sr. M. Veronica Johnson
Sr. M. Ricarda Kavanagh, RN
Sr. Lydia Kelly
Sr. M. Edmund Kennedy
Sr. Irene Kennedy
Sr. M. Kevin Kennedy
Sr. Margaret Kennedy, RN
Sr. M. Xaverius (Catherine) Kenny, RN
Sr. M. Adrienne Keough
Sr. M. Brenda Lacey, RN
Sr. Elsie Lahey
Sr. M. Raphael Lane
Sr. M. St. Clare Maddigan, RN
Sr. Marian Grace Manning, RN
Sr. Mary Manning, RN
Sr. Elizabeth Marrie
Sr. M. Alacoque McDonald
Sr. M. Vincent McDonald
Sr. M. St. Joan McDonnell, RN

Sr. Jane McGrath, RN
Sr. M. Julia McGrath, RN
Sr. M. Loretta McIsaac, RN
Sr. M. Teresita McNamee, RN (USA)
Sr. M. Ignatius Molloy
Sr. Betty Morrissey
Sr. M. Assisium Murphy
Sr. Margaret Murphy, RN
Sr. Marie Aiden Murphy
Sr. Colette Nagle
Sr. M. Virginia Nash, RN
Sr. Irene Neville
Sr. M. St. John Norris, RN
Sr. M. Faustina O'Brien, RN
Sr. M. Rosarii O'Brien, RN
Sr. M. St. Jude O'Grady, RN
Sr. Madonna O'Neill
Sr. M. Gerard O'Reilly
Sr. M. Stanislaus Parsons, RN
Sr. Eileen Penney, RN
Sr. Ida Pomroy, RN
Sr. M. Thomasina Pomroy
Sr. Lorraine Power, MD
Sr. M. Calasanctius Power, RN
Sr. M. Carmelita Power
Sr. M. Lucy Power, RN
Sr. M. Rose Power
Sr. M. Aloysius Rawlins, RN
Sr. M. Anita Reddy
Sr. M. Bonaventure Reddy
Sr. M. Philippa Reddy
Sr. M. Callista Ryan, RNA
Sr. M. Eleanor Savage
Sr. M. Imelda Smith

Sr. Diane Smyth
Sr. M. Alexius St. George
Sr. Margaret Mary St. John
Sr. M. Andrea Sutton
Sr. Mary Tarrant, RN
Sr. M. Audrey Tobin, RN
Sr. M. Francis Xavier Turpin
Sr. M. Liguori Wade
Sr. Loretta Walsh, RN
Sr. Mary Walsh
Sr. M. Loyola Whelan
Sr. Imelda White, RN
Sr. Margaret Williams
Sr. M. Raymond Woodrow

Weekly Ministry
Sr. M. Edward Hodge (Music)
Sr. M. Celine Veitch (Music)

Summer Ministry
Sr. Ruth Beresford
Sr. Barbara Kenny
Sr. Alice Mackey
Sr. Nellie Pomroy

Appendix B

St. Clare's Mercy Hospital

Members of the Board of Directors
1939-1940

Sr. M. Bridget O'Connor

Ms. Marcella O'Connor

Sr. M. Stanislaus Parsons

Sr. M. Aloysius Rawlins

Archbishop Edward P. Roche

Members of the Board of Governors
1956-1995

Miss Irene Baird

Dr. George W. Battcock

Mrs. Eleanor Bonnell

Mrs. Priscilla Boutcher

Mr. Francis Brennan

Mr. John Brophy

Dr. Garrett M. Brownrigg

Sr. Marion Collins

Dr. Sean Conroy

Sr. Phyllis Corbett

Rev. Raymond Corriveau

Mr. Roger Crosbie

Sr. Elizabeth Davis

Sr. M. Hildegarde Dunphy

Mr. James Fagan

Mr. Francis Fitzgerald

Mr. Hubert Furey

Honourable R. S. Furlong

Miss Roseanne Grant

Sr. Helen Harding

Mrs. Catherine Henley

Sr M. Fabian Hennebury

Mr Brian Higgins

Judge J. G. Horan

Mr. David Howley

Monsignor G. H. Hull

Miss Sharon Keiley

Sr. M. Xaverius (Catherine) Kenny (Sect.)

Archbishop James MacDonald

Sr. M. St. Clare Maddigan

Monsignor Edward Maher

Sr. Patricia Maher

Sr. Patricia March

Mr. Aidan Maloney

Mr. Cyril McCormack

Mr. Earl McCurdy

Dr. David McCutcheon

Monsignor Richard T. McGrath

Sr. M. Loretta McIsaac

Dr. E. Aidan McLaughlin

Mrs. Elizabeth Morgan

Monsignor David Morrissey

Monsignor R. McDermott Murphy

Monsignor D. L. O'Keefe

Mr. John O'Neill

Mr. Raymond O'Neill

Mr. Thomas O'Reilly

Mr. Jay Parker

Dr. David Peddle

Archbishop Alphonsus Penney

Mr. E. J. Phelan

Sr. M. Lucy Power

Sr. Marie Michael Power

Dr. Gregory Russell

Dr. E. L. Sharpe

Miss Ada Simms

Dr. Robert J. Simms

Mr. John Sinnott

Archbishop P. J. Skinner

Sr. M. Imelda Smith

Sr. M. Alexius St. George

Monsignor Harold A. Summers

Dr. Ian C. K. Tough

Sr. M. Assumpta Veitch

Mr. John Walsh

Mr. Ray Walsh

Monsignor Roderick T. White

Dr. Gordon Winter

Judge Joseph A. Woodrow

Appendix C

St. Clare's Mercy Hospital

Mission Statements

MISSION STATEMENT 1991

St. Clare's Mercy Hospital is a Catholic institution dedicated to the healing ministry of Jesus and the church. To carry out this mandate, St. Clare's Mercy Hospital strives to be faithful to the mission and values of Jesus, and to witness to His spirit, particularly His mercy and compassion. The hospital's motto, Mercy Above All, calls volunteers, staff including physicians, the Board of Governors, and the Sisters of Mercy, through their collaborative efforts, to care for the sick and dying with competence and compassion, and without discrimination. This mission affirms the dignity and uniqueness of each person, fosters holistic healing, and promotes the pastoral care of all patients. The hospital commits itself to all who serve within the hospital community and seeks to provide an environment of recognition, care and support. Inherent in the mission of St. Clare's Mercy Hospital is a commitment to health promotion and disease prevention, and the promotion of a healthy social and physical environment. The hospital recognizes a strong ethical dimension in carrying out its mission; it supports and complies with the ethical standards outlined in the health care ethics guidelines of the Canadian Conference of Bishops.

MISSION STATEMENT 1994

The mission, values and philosophy of St. Clare's Mercy Hospital are carried out in the spirit and tradition of the Sisters of Mercy. St. Clare's motto, "Mercy Above All," calls volunteers, staff, including physicians, the Advisory Council, and the Sisters of Mercy, through their collaborative efforts, to care for the sick and dying with competence and compassion, and without discrimination. This mission affirms the dignity and uniqueness of each person, fosters holistic healing, and promotes the pastoral care of all patients. St. Clare's commits itself to all who serve within the hospital community and seeks to provide an environment of recognition, care and support. Inherent in the mission of St. Clare's Mercy Hospital is a commitment to health promotion and disease prevention, and the promotion of a healthy social and physical environment. St. Clare's recognizes a strong ethical dimension in carrying out its mission.

APPENDIX D

St. Clare's Mercy Hospital

Educational Affiliations 1995 (at the time preceding the assimilation of St. Clare's Mercy Hospital into the Health Care Corporation of St. John's)

Salvation Army Grace General Hospital
- School of Nursing

The St. John's General Hospital
- School of Nursing

Memorial University
- Faculty of Medicine
- School of Nursing
- Faculty of Business Administration and Commerce
- Faculty of Engineering and Applied Science
- School of Social Work
- Faculty of Science (Psychology)
- School of Pharmacy

Dalhousie University (Halifax, Nova Scotia)
- Department of Physiotherapy
- Department of Occupational Therapy

Cabot Institute of Trades and Technology
- Laboratory Technology Program
- X-ray Technology Program
- Nursing Assistant Program
- Secretarial Science
- Computer Studies
- Biomedical Technology
- Certified Engineering Technology

Private Post-secondary Schools
   - Secretarial Studies
Association of Registered Nurses of Newfoundland
   - Grant McEwan College (RN Refresher)
THERAPEIA
Catholic Health Association of Canada
Newfoundland Hospital Association
Canadian Hospital Association
Catholic Hospital Association of the United States of America

Appendix E

In the House of Assembly on December 8, 1994, the Honourable Lloyd Matthews, minister of health, announced the agreement between the Sisters of Mercy and the Government of Newfoundand and Labrador. The following is the ministerial statement.

Ministerial Statement

Government and Congregation of Sisters of Mercy Reach Agreement on the future of St. Clare's Mercy Hospital

Mr. Speaker, I am pleased to advise the House that earlier today Sister Marion Collins, Superior General of the Congregation of the Sisters of Mercy, on behalf of the Congregation, and I, on behalf of the Government, signed an Agreement respecting the future of St. Clare's Mercy Hospital. This Agreement was negotiated over the past year by representatives of the Sisters of Mercy, the Board of Governors of St. Clare's, and senior Government officials.

Under the Agreement, the Government has purchased the St. Clare's Mercy Hospital property which will be operated under the direction of the new St. John's Hospitals Board [Health Care Corporation of St. John's] announced earlier in the year. The Agreement provides for the Sisters of Mercy to continue to carry out their ministry of health care at St. Clare's. It also provides that the mission, philosophy, and values and ethical principles of St. Clare's Mercy Hospital will be maintained within the new

Board structure. The title to St. Clare's Mercy Hospital will be transferred to the Province, and governance of the Hospital will be with the new Hospital Board.

Mr. Speaker, the Government has purchased the St. Clare's Mercy Hospital property for $6.5 million, which will be amortized as to principal and interest over a period of 20 years. The purchase price, while recognizing the value of the land and the direct financial input of the Sisters of Mercy into the St. Clare's property, cannot in any way be projected as representing the value of the significant contribution which the Sisters have made to health services in this Province, or the current replacement cost of St. Clare's.

Mr. Speaker, I believe that this Agreement is in the best interest of the people of the Province, and I want to thank the Sisters of Mercy for the vision they demonstrated in their negotiations with Government. Their willingness to relinquish the title and control of St. Clare's Mercy Hospital and allow it to continue as one of the leading health care institutions in our Province reflects their deep commitment to the health care system and to seeing St. Clare's continue as an integral part of the new regional board structure in St. John's.

At this time, Mr. Speaker, I would be remiss if I did not pay tribute to the Congregation of the Sisters of Mercy for the tremendous contribution they have made to health care services in the Province during the past 72 years. The people of this Province have benefitted immeasurably from that contribution. It is my hope and expectation that the Sisters of Mercy will continue to contribute to the health care system of the Province through St. Clare's Mercy Hospital and that the people of our Province will continue to benefit from their ministry in health care.

December 8, 1994

Bibliography

Archival Sources

Archives of the Archdiocese of St. John's
Archives of the City of St. John's
Archives of the Presentation Sisters, St. John's
Archives of the Sisters of Mercy, Baltimore, Maryland, USA
Archives of the Sisters of Mercy, St. John's
Library of St. Clare's Mercy Hospital, St. John's

Newspapers

The Daily News
The Evening Telegram
The Express
The Monitor
Patriot and Terra Nova Herald
The Sunday Express
The Telegram

Journals

Inter Nos
Journal of the House of Assembly
Mercy Communico

Secondary Sources

Beaton, Marilyn, and Jeanette Walsh. *From the Voices of Nurses: An Oral History of Newfoundland Nurses Who Graduated Prior to 1950.* St. John's: Jesperson Publishing, 2004.

Bellamy, Kathrine E. *Weavers of the Tapestry.* St. John's: Flanker Press, 2006.

Burke, Catherine Kirby. *Residence Recollections and Hospital Happenings.* St. John's: n.p., 1999.

Cadigan, Sean. "The Second World War, 1939-1945." Newfoundland and Labrador Heritage. http://www.heritage.nf.ca/law/wwii.html.

Carroll, Mary Austin. *Leaves from the Annals of the Sisters of Mercy.* Vol. 3, *Newfoundland and the United States.* New York: Catholic Publication Society, 1883.

Daley, Katherine. *Health Services in Newfoundland & Labrador: Timeline, 1662-2004.* St. John's: Newfoundland and Labrador Health and Community Services Archive and Museum, 2004.

Darcy, Brother J. B. *Fire Upon the Earth: The Life and Times of Bishop Michael Fleming, O.S.F..* St. John's: Creative Book Publishing, 2003.

Eliot, T. S. "Choruses from 'The Rock' X." In *A Guide to the Selected Poems of T. S. Eliot,* 6th ed., by B. C. Southam, 256. New York: Barnes and Noble, 1970.

Encyclopedia of Newfoundland and Labrador. 5 vols. St. John's: Newfoundland Book Publishers and Harry Cuff Publications, 1981-1994.

Hennebury, Sister M. Fabian. "St. Clare's Mercy Hospital, 1922-1982." Unpublished manuscript. Archives of the Sisters of Mercy, St. John's.

Higgins, Jenny: "19th-Century Health Care." Newfoundland and Labrador Heritage. http://www.heritage.nf.ca/ society/19c_health.html.

Hogan, Sister M. Williamina. *Pathways of Mercy: History of the Foundation of the Sisters of Mercy in Newfoundland, 1842-1984.* St. John's: Harry Cuff Publications, 1986.

Howley, Very Reverend M. F. *Ecclesiastical History of Newfoundland.* Boston: Doyle and Whittle, 1888.

Nevitt, Joyce. *White Caps and Black Bands: Nursing in Newfoundland to 1934.* St. John's: Jesperson Press, 1978.

Nolan, Stephen M. *A History of Health Care in Newfoundland and Labrador.* St. John's: Newfoundland and Labrador Health and Community Services Archive and Museum, 2004.

O'Mara, John F. "I Swear By Apollo: Irish Physicians and Surgeons in Newfoundland and Labrador before 1900." Lecture to the Irish Newfoundland Association, St. John's, November 17, 2002.

O'Neill, Paul. *The Oldest City: The Story of St. John's, Newfoundland.* Portugal Cove-St. Philip's, NL: Boulder Publications, 2003.

Power, Sister Mary Calasanctius. "The St. Clare's Mercy Hospital School of Nursing, 1939–1979." Unpublished manuscript. Archives of the Sisters of Mercy, St. John's, 1979.

St. Clare's Mercy Hospital. *St. Clare's Mercy Hospital, 1922–1947.* Silver Jubilee Booklet. St. John's: n.p., 1947.

——. *St. Clare's Mercy Hospital, St. John's, Newfoundland, 1922–1961.* St. John's: n.p., 1961.

——. *St. Clare's Mercy Hospital, Historical Highlights, 1922–1972.* St. John's: n.p., 1972.

——. *St. Clare's Mercy Hospital, St. John's, Newfoundland, 1922–1982, 60th Anniversary Historical Highlights.* St. John's: n.p., 1982.

——. *St. Clare's Mercy Hospital, Historical Highlights, 1922–1998.* St. John's: n.p., 1998.

——. *The Claretian, Golden Jubilee St. Clare's Mercy Hospital School of Nursing 1939–1989.* St. John's: n.p., 1998.

INDEX

ABOUT THE AUTHOR

Kathrine E. Bellamy, RSM, was born in Bay Roberts to parents William and Katherine (O'Flynn) Bellamy and had one brother, William. Sister Kathrine received her early education at St. Matthew's Anglican School. At the age of twelve, she boarded at St. Bride's College, Littledale, St. John's, where she completed high school and then went on to Mount Saint Vincent University in Halifax. When she was eighteen, she entered the Congregation of the Sisters of Mercy of Newfoundland. After her profession, she was assigned to Our Lady of Mercy School, Military Road, St. John's, where she began her career as a music teacher. Sister Kathrine is recognized mainly for her work with the school choirs at the Immaculate Conception Academy, Bell Island, and at Our Lady of Mercy School and Holy Heart of Mary High School, St. John's. Under her direction, Our Lady of Mercy Glee Club received many awards, and it was the first Newfoundland choir to win the Mathieson Trophy for the best junior choir in Canada. By coincidence, one of her former pupils, Margo Cranford, is the publisher of this book!

In addition to her work in the schools, Sister Kathrine was organist and choir director at the Basilica of St. John the Baptist, a position she held for twenty-four years. In 1984, Sister Kathrine directed an archdiocesan choir for the visit of Pope John Paul II to the basilica where, in addition to her duties as music director, she was deeply involved in the parish outreach to the poor.

In May 2006, Sister Kathrine was awarded the degree of

doctor of laws, *honoris causa,* by Memorial University, St. John's, Newfoundland and Labrador. In December 2006, Sister Kathrine was invested into the Order of Newfoundland and Labrador by the Honourable Edward Roberts, lieutenant governor of Newfoundland and Labrador. In February 2007, Sister Kathrine was appointed to the Order of Canada by Her Excellency the Right Honourable Michaëlle Jean, governor general of Canada.

Throughout her life, Sister Kathrine kept in touch with her former pupils, especially the "Mercy girls," and with her only nephew, the Very Reverend William J. Bellamy, former rector of the Anglican Cathedral and dean of the Anglican Diocese of Eastern Newfoundland and Labrador, and his family.